Benjamin Disraeli

Inaugural Address Delivered to the University of Glasgow

Nov. 19, 1873

Second Edition

Benjamin Disraeli

Inaugural Address Delivered to the University of Glasgow Nov. 19, 1873
Second Edition

ISBN/EAN: 9783337084622

Printed in Europe, USA, Canada, Australia, Japan

Cover: Foto ©ninafisch / pixelio.de

More available books at **www.hansebooks.com**

INAUGURAL ADDRESS

DELIVERED TO THE

UNIVERSITY OF GLASGOW

November 19, 1873

BY THE

RIGHT HON. BENJAMIN DISRAELI, M.P.

LORD RECTOR OF THE UNIVERSITY OF GLASGOW

SECOND EDITION

INCLUDING THE

OCCASIONAL SPEECHES AT GLASGOW

AUTHORISED EDITION, CORRECTED BY THE AUTHOR

LONDON
LONGMANS, GREEN, AND CO.
1873

PREFACE.

The Publishers having informed me that there is a demand for the occasional Speeches made by me during the recent visit to Glasgow, I avail myself of the second edition of the 'Inaugural Address' to comply with their wish that they should be added to it. D.

Hughenden:
December 4, 1873.

INAUGURAL ADDRESS DELIVERED AT THE COLLEGE OF GLASGOW, NOVEMBER 19, 1873.

MR. PRINCIPAL, PROFESSORS, AND STUDENTS—

MY first duty, and my deepest gratification, is to thank you for the honour which you conferred on me two years ago. It is a high one. No one can be insensible to sympathy from the unknown, but the pleasure is necessarily heightened when it is offered by the educated and refined; when that body is representative, and, above all, when it represents the youth of a famous country.

My next duty, and one of which the fulfilment is scarcely less gratifying, is to avail myself of the privilege attendant on the office to which you have raised me, and to offer you some observations either on the course of your studies or the conduct of your lives, which, if made by me, will be made without pretence or presumption, quite satisfied if, when we are separated, any chance remark of mine may recur to your

B

memory, and lead you to not altogether unprofitable meditation.

Were I to follow my own bent, I would dwell on those delightful studies which occupy a considerable portion of your time within your academic halls, studies which, while they form your taste and strengthen your intelligence, will prove to you in future years both a guide and a consolation; but when I recollect the illustrious roll of those who have preceded me in this office, and remember how fully and how recently many of them have devoted their genius and their learning to such an enterprise, I am inclined to think that the field, though in my opinion inexhaustible, has been for the present sufficiently cultivated, and that as you are about to enter life at a period which promises, or rather which threatens, to be momentous, it would not be inappropriate were I to make some observations which may tend to assist you in your awaiting trials.

He who would succeed in life, and obtain that position to which his character and capacity entitle him, has need of two kinds of knowledge. It would seem at the first blush that self-knowledge were not very difficult of attainment. If there be any subject on which a person can arrive at accurate conclusions, it should be his own disposition and his own talents. But it is not so. The period of youth in this respect is one of great doubt and difficulty. It is a period alike of false confidence and unreasonable distrust, of perplexity, of despondency, and sometimes of despair. It has been said by an eminent physician that there are very few persons of either sex who have attained their eighteenth year who have not contemplated withdrawing from the world—withdrawing from that world which, in fact, they have never entered. Doubtless, this morbid feeling is occasioned in a great degree by a dread of the unknown, but it is also much to be attributed to, and it certainly is heightened by, an ignorance of themselves.

How, then, is this self-knowledge to be acquired, and where are we to obtain assistance in this quest? From the family circle? Its incompetency in this respect is a proverb. Perception of character is always a rare gift, but around the domestic hearth it is almost unknown. Every one is acquainted with the erroneous estimates of their offspring which have been made even by illustrious parents. The silent, but perhaps pensive, boy is looked upon as a dullard, while the flippancy of youth in a commonplace character is interpreted into a dangerous vivacity which may in time astonish, perhaps even alarm, the world. A better criterion should be found in the judgment of contemporaries who are our equals. But the generous ardour of youth is not favourable to critical discrimination. Its sympathy is quick, it admires and applauds; but it lavishes its applause and admiration on qualities which are often not intrinsically important, and it always exaggerates. And thus it is that the hero of school and of college often disappoints expectation in after life. The truth is, he has shown no deficiency in the qualities which obtained him his early repute, but he has been wanting in the capacity adapted to subsequent opportunities.

Some are of opinion that the surest judge of youthful character must be the tutor. And there is a passage in Isocrates on this head not without interest. He was an accomplished instructor, and he tells us he always studied to discover the bent of those who attended his lectures. So, after due observation, he would say to one, 'You are intended for action, and the camp is the life which will become you;' to another 'You should cultivate poetry;' a third was adapted to the passionate exercitations of the Pnyx; while a fourth was clearly destined for the groves and porticoes of philosophy. The early Jesuits, who were masters of education, were accustomed to keep secret registers of their observations on their pupils, and generations afterwards, when these records were examined, it is said the happy prescience of their remarks was strikingly proved by the subsequent success of many who had attained fame in arts and arms. But the Jesuits, gentlemen, whatever they may be now, were then very clever men; and I must confess that I am doubtful whether the judgment of tutors in general would be as infallible as that of Isocrates.

In the first place, a just perception of character is always a rare gift. When possessed in a high degree it is the quality which specially indicates the leader of men. It is that which enables a General or a Minister to select the fit instrument for the public purpose; without which all the preparations for a campaign, however costly and complete, may be fruitless, and all the deliberations of councils and all the discussions of Parliament prove mere dust and wind. Scholars and philosophers are in general too much absorbed by their own peculiar studies or pursuits to be skilled in the discrimination of character, and if the aptitude of a pupil is recognised by them, it is generally when he has evinced a disposition to excel in some branch of acquirement which has established their own celebrity.

No, gentlemen, I believe, after all, it will be found that it is best and inevitable, in the pursuit of self-knowledge, that we should depend on self-communion. Unquestionably, where there is a strong predisposition, it will assert itself in spite of all obstacles, but even here only after an initiation of many errors and much self-deception. One of the fruitful sources of that self-deception is to be found in the susceptibility of the youthful mind. The sympathy is so quick that we are apt to transfer to our own persons the qualities which we admire in others. If it be the age of a great poet, his numbers are for ever resounding in our ears, and we sigh for his laurels; if a military age, nothing will content us but to be at the head of armies; if an age of oratory and politics, our spirit requires that we should be leaders of parties and Ministers of State. In some instances the predisposition may be true, but it is in the nature of things that the instances must be rare. In ninety-nine cases out of one hundred the feeling is not idiosyncratic but mimetic, and we have mistaken a quick sensibility for creative power. Then comes to a young man the period of disappointment and despondency. To publish poems which no one will read; to make speeches to which no one will listen; after reveries of leading armies and directing councils, to find yourself, on your entrance into the business of life, incapable of influencing the conduct of an ordinary individual,—all this is bitter; but all depends upon how the lesson is received. A weak spirit will not survive this catastrophe of his self-love. He will sink into chronic despondency, and, without attempting to rally, he will pass through life as a phantom, and be remembered, as an old man, only by the golden promise of his deceptive youth. But a man of sense will accept these consequences, however apparently mortifying, with courage and candour. He will dive into his own intelligence, he will analyse the circumstances of his failure, he will discriminate how much was occasioned by indigenous deficiencies, and how much may be attributed to external and fortuitous circumstances. And in this severe introspection he may obtain that self-knowledge he requires; his failures may be the foundation of his ultimate success, and in this moral and intellectual struggle he may discover the true range of his powers, and the right bent of his character and capacity.

So much, gentlemen, for self-knowledge, a subject that for ages has furnished philosophers with treatises. I do not pretend to be a philosopher, and I have not offered you a treatise, but I have made some remarks which are, at least, the result of my own observation.

But assuming that you have at length attained this indispensable self-knowledge, and that you have an opportunity, in the pursuits of life, of following the bent of your disposition, we come now to the second and not less important condition of success in life: have you that other kind of knowledge which is required?—do you comprehend the spirit of the age in which your faculties are to be exercised? Hitherto you have been as explorers in a mountain district. You have surveyed and examined valleys, you have penetrated gorges, you have crossed many a ridge and range, till at length, having overcome all obstacles, you have reached the crest of the commanding height, and, like the soldiers of Xenophon, you behold the sea. But the sea that you behold is the Ocean of Life! In what vessels are you going to embark? With what instruments are you furnished? What is the port of your destination?

It is singular that though there is no lack of those who will explain the past, and certainly no want of those who will predict the future, when the present is concerned— the present that we see and feel—our opinions about it are in general bewildered and mistaken. And yet, without this acquaintance with the spirit of the age in which we live, whatever our culture and whatever our opportunities, it is probable that our lives may prove a blunder. When the young King of Macedon decided that the time had arrived when Europe should invade Asia, he recognised the spirit of his age. The revelations of the weakness of the Great King, which had been made during the immortal expedition of the Ten Thousand, and still more during the campaigns of Agesilaus, had gradually formed a public opinion which Alexander dared to represent. When Caius Julius perceived that the colossal empire formed by the Senate and populace of Rome could not be sustained on the municipal institutions of a single city, however illustrious, he understood the spirit of the age. Constantine understood the spirit of his age when he recognised the Sign under which he was resolved to conquer. I think that Luther recognised the spirit of the age when he nailed his Theses against Indulgences to the gates of a Thuringian church. The great Princes of the House of Tudor, and the statesmen they employed, were all persons who understood the spirit of their age.

But it may be said, 'These are heroic instances. A perception of the spirit of their age may be necessary to the success of princes and statesmen, but is not needful, or equally needful, for those of lesser degree.' I think there would be fallacy in this criticism, and that the necessity of this knowledge pervades the whole business of life. Take, for example, the choice of a profession; a knowledge of the spirit of the age may save a young man from embracing a profession which the spirit of the age dooms to become obsolete. It is the same with the pursuits of commerce. This knowledge may guard a man from embarking his capital in a decaying trade, or from forming connexions and even establishments in countries from which the spirit of the age is gradually diverting all commercial transactions. I would say a knowledge of the spirit of the age is necessary for every public man, and in a country like ours, where the subject is called upon hourly to exercise rights and to fulfil duties which, in however small a degree, go to the aggregate of that general sentiment which ultimately governs States, every one is a public man, although he may not be a public character.

But it does not follow, because the spirit of the age is perceived and recognised, it should be embraced and followed, or even that success in life depends upon adopting it. What I wished to impress upon you was that success in life depended on comprehending it. The spirit of the age may be an unsound and injurious spirit; it may be the moral duty of a man, not only not to defer to, but to resist it, and if it be unsound and injurious, in so doing he will not only fulfil his duty, but he may accomplish his success in life. The spirit of the age, for instance, was in favour of the Crusades. They occasioned a horrible havoc of human life; they devastated Asia and exhausted Europe; and, in all probability, in acting in this instance according to the spirit of the age, a man would have forfeited his life, and certainly wasted his estate, with no further satisfaction than having massacred some Jews and slain some Saracens.

What then, gentlemen, is the spirit of the age in which we ourselves live; of that world which in a few years, more or less, you will have all entered; where you are to establish yourselves in life; where you have to encounter in that object every conceivable difficulty; perplexities of judgment, material obstacles, tests of all your qualities, and searching trials of your character; and all these circumstances more or less affected by the spirit of the age, an acquaintance with which will assist you in forming your decisions and in guiding your course?

It appears to me that I should not greatly err were I to describe the spirit of this age as the spirit of equality; but 'equality' is a word of wide import, under which various schools of thought may assemble and yet arrive at different and even contradictory conclusions. I hold that Civil equality—that is, equality of all subjects before the law, and that a law which recognises the personal rights of all subjects—is the only foundation of a perfect commonwealth—one which secures to all liberty, order, and justice. The principle of Civil equality has long prevailed in this kingdom. It has been applied during the last half-century more finely and completely to the constantly and largely varying circumstances of the country; but it had prevailed more or less in Britain for centuries, and I attribute the patriotism of our population mainly to this circumstance, and I believe that it has had more to do with the security of the soil than those geographical attributes usually enlarged upon.

Another land, long our foe, but now our rival only in the arts of peace, thought fit, at the end of the last century, to reconstruct its social system, and to rebuild it on the principle of Social equality. To effect this object it was prepared to make, and it made, great sacrifices. It subverted all the institutions of the country: a Monarchy of 800 years whose traditionary and systematic policy had created the kingdom; a National Church—for, though Romanist, it had secured its liberties; a tenure of land which maintained a valiant nobility, that never can be restored; it confiscated all endowments, and abolished all corporations;

erased from the map of the soil all the ancient divisions, and changed the landmarks and very name of the country. Indeed, it entirely effected its purpose, which was to destroy all the existing social elements and level the past to the dust. This experiment has had fair play, and you can judge of its results by the experience of eighty years.

It is not in Scotland that the name of France will ever be mentioned without affection, and I will not yield to any Scotchman in my appreciation of the brilliant qualities and the resplendent achievements of its gifted people. We are not blind to their errors, but their calamities are greater than their errors, and their merits are greater than their calamities. When I heard that their bright city was beleaguered, and that the breach was in the wall, I confess I felt that pang which I remember, as a child, I always experienced when I read of Lysander entering the City of the Violet Crown. But, gentlemen, I may on this occasion be permitted to say that of all the many services which France has rendered to Europe—Europe, that land of ancient creeds and ancient Governments, and manners and customs older than both—not the least precious is the proof she has afforded to us that the principle of Social equality is not one on which a nation can safely rely in the hour of trial and in the day of danger. Then it is found that there is no one to lead and nothing to rally round. There is not a man in the country who can assemble fifty people. And rightly : since for an individual to direct is an usurpation of the sovereignty of the many. Those who ought to lead, feel isolated, and those who wish to obey know not to whom to proffer their devotion. All personal influences are dead. All depends on the Central Government, a sufficient power in fair weather, but in stormy times generally that part of the machine which first breaks.

Civil equality prevails in Britain, and Social equality prevails in France. The essence of civil equality is to abolish privilege; the essence of social equality is to destroy classes. If the principle of equality at the present day assumed only these two forms, I do not think there would be much to perplex you in your choice, or in your judgment as to their respective results. But that is not so. The equality which is now sought by vast multitudes of men in many countries, which is enforced by writers not deficient in logic, in eloquence, and even learning, scarcely deigns to recognise civil equality, and treats social equality only as an obsolete truth. No moral or metaphysical elements will satisfy them. They demand physical and material equality. This is the disturbing spirit which is now rising like a moaning wind in Europe, and which, when you enter the world, may possibly be a raging storm. It may, therefore, be as well that your attention should be called to its nature, and that you may be led to consider its consequences.

The leading principle of this new school is that there is no happiness which is not material, and that every living being has a right to a share in that physical welfare. The first obstacle to their purpose is found in the rights of private property. Therefore, they must be abolished. But the social system must be established on some principle; and, therefore, for the rights of property they would substitute the rights of labour. Now, the rights of labour cannot be fully enjoyed if there be any limit to employment. The great limit to employment, to the rights of labour, and to the physical and material equality of man, is found in the division of the world into states and nations. Thus, as civil equality would abolish privilege, social equality would destroy classes; so material and physical equality strikes at the principle of patriotism, and is prepared to abrogate countries.

Now I am addressing a race of men who are proud, and justly proud, of their country. I know not that the sentiment of patriotism beats in any breast more strongly than in that of a Scotchman. Neither time nor distance, I believe, enfeebles that passion. It is as vehement on the banks of the Ganges as on the banks of the Clyde, and in the speculative turmoil of Melbourne as in the bustling energy of Glasgow. Why is a Scotchman proud of his country? Because the remembrance of it awakes a tradition of heroic exploits and inspiring emotions; of sacrifices for its sake in the field and on the scaffold; of high examples of military skill and civil prudence; of literary and scientific fame; of commanding eloquence and profound philosophy, and of fascinating poesy and romance; all of which a Scotchman feels ennoble his existence, and all of which he is conscious have inevitably sprung from the circumstances of his native land. So that the very configuration of the soil and the temper of the clime have influenced his private virtues and his public life, as they unquestionably have given a form and colour to those works of creative genius which have gained the sympathy and admiration of the world.

No, gentlemen, it is not true that the only real happiness is physical happiness; it is not true that physical happiness is the highest happiness; it is not true that physical happiness is a principle on which you can build up a flourishing and enduring commonwealth. A civilised community must rest on a large realised capital of thought and sentiment; there must be a reserved fund of public morality to draw upon in the exigencies of national life. Society has a soul as well as a body. The traditions of a nation are part of its existence. Its valour and its discipline, its religious faith, its venerable laws, its science and erudition, its poetry, its art, its eloquence and its scholarship, are as much portions of its life as its agriculture, its commerce, and its engineering skill. Nay, I would go further, I would say that without these qualities material excellence cannot be attained.

But, gentlemen, the new philosophy strikes further than at the existence of patriotism   It strikes at the home; it strikes at the individuality of man. It would reduce civilised society to human flocks and herds. That it may produce in your time much disturbance, possibly much destruction, I pretend not to deny; but I must express my conviction that it will not ultimately triumph. I hold that the main obstacles to its establishment are to be found in human nature itself. They are both physical and moral. If it be true, as I believe, that an aristocracy distinguished merely by wealth must perish from satiety, so I hold it is equally true that a people who recognise no higher aim than physical enjoyment must become selfish and enervated. Under such circumstances the supremacy of race, which is the key of history, will assert itself. Some human progeny, distinguished by their bodily vigour or their masculine intelligence, or by both qualities, will assert their superiority, and conquer a world which deserves to be enslaved. It will then be found that our boasted progress has only been an advancement in a circle, and that our new philosophy has brought us back to that old serfdom which it has taken ages to extirpate.

But the still more powerful—indeed, I hold the insurmountable—obstacle to the establishment of the new opinions will be furnished by the essential elements of the human mind. Our idiosyncracy is not bounded by the planet which we inhabit. We can investigate space and we can comprehend eternity. No considerations limited to this sphere have hitherto furnished the excitement which man requires, or the sanctions for his conduct which his nature imperatively demands. The spiritual nature of man is stronger than Codes or Constitutions. No Government can endure which does not recognise that for its foundation, and no legislation last which does not flow from this fountain. The principle may develope itself in manifold forms—shape of many Creeds and many Churches; but the principle is divine. As time is divided into day and night, so religion rests upon the providence of God and the responsibility of man. One is manifest, the other mysterious; but both are facts. Nor is there, as some would teach you, anything in these convictions which tends to contract our intelligence or our sympathies. On the contrary, religion invigorates the intellect and expands the heart. He who has a due sense of his relations to God is best qualified to fulfil his duties to man. A fine writer of antiquity—perhaps the finest—has recorded in a beautiful passage his belief in Divine Providence, and in the necessity of universal toleration:—

"'Εγὼ μὲν οὖν, καὶ ταῦτα, καὶ τὰ πάντ' ἀεὶ,
Φάσκοιμ' ἂν ἀνθρώποισι μηχανᾶν θεούς·
Ὅτῳ δὲ μὴ τάδ' ἐστὶν ἐν γνώμῃ φίλα,
Κεῖνός τ' ἐκεῖνα στοργέτω, κἀγὼ τάδε.'

These lines were written, more than two thousand years ago, by the most Attic of Athenian poets. In the perplexities of life I have sometimes found in them a solace and a satisfaction; and I now deliver them to you, to guide your consciences and to guard your lives.

SPEECH AT THE BANQUET GIVEN BY THE CITY OF GLASGOW TO THE LORD RECTOR ON THE SAME DAY.

MR. DISRAELI, who on rising to return thanks was loudly cheered, said—

MY LORD PROVOST AND GENTLEMEN,—I must thank you most cordially for the kind manner in which you have received the toast which his Lordship has just proposed, and for the courteous and munificent hospitality you have extended to me, without any reference to political opinion, as the Lord Provost has very properly intimated.

I have always thought it to be one of the happiest circumstances of public life in England that we have not permitted our political opinions to interfere with our social enjoyments. I believe it is a characteristic of the country; at least, I am not aware that it is shared by any other. For instance, if you are on the Continent and wish to pay your respects to a Minister and go to his Reception, you are invited by the Minister. The consequence is you find no one there except those who follow him. It is not so in England. I remember some years ago meeting under the charming roof of one of the most accomplished women of the time the most celebrated diplomatist of certainly this half century, and he said to me, 'What a wonderful system of society you have in England! I have not been on speaking terms with Lord Palmerston for three weeks, and yet here I am; but you see I am paying a visit to Lady Palmerston.'

It is unnecessary to dwell now on what may be the causes that produce this happy state of society in this country, which is essentially a political country, and therefore the circumstance is more to be valued. At the same time there is no doubt that by mixing together with this freedom both parties become acquainted with some political traits with which they might not otherwise be conversant. I did not know until to-night, for example, when we have heard it from a great authority, that it was a leading principle of the Liberal party not to give their opponents credit either for talents or patriotism. I may have heard it before, but I thought it must be the assertion of some malignant Tory. What I wish to say for the Conservative party is that it is not the principle which we adopt. We all give our opponents credit for the greatest abilities and the best intentions, although we may intimate our occasional regret that those abilities are misapplied, and that, whatever may be their good intentions, they meet that destiny which is proverbially provided for that kind of article.

Gentlemen, I thank you for the kindness with which you have received the intimation of the Lord Provost with regard to my own political career. I would not trouble you with touching on it further, but after the allusion which has been made perhaps you will permit me to say that it has been my fortune to be the leader in the House of Commons of one of the great parties of the State for twenty-five years, and that there is no record, I believe, in the Parliamentary history of the country of the duration of a leadership equal to it. There have been in my time two illustrious instances of the great parties being led by most eminent men; one was the instance of Sir Robert Peel, who led the Tory party for eighteen years, though unfortunately it twice broke asunder; there was also the instance of one who is still spared to us, and who, I hope, will be long spared to us, for he is the pride of this country as he was the honour of the House of Commons—Lord John Russell. He led one of the great parties seventeen years, though at last it slipped out of his hands.

Do not suppose I make these observations in any vain spirit. The reason why I have been able to lead any party for such a period, and under circumstances of some difficulty and discouragement, is that the party with which I am connected is really the most generous and the most indulgent party that ever existed. I cannot help smiling sometimes when I hear of those convenient intimations given by those, who know all the secrets of the political world, of the extreme anxiety of the Conservative party to get rid of my services. The fact is, the Conservative party can get rid of my services whenever they give me any intimation that such is their desire. All I can say is, whenever I have desired to relieve them of it, they have only too kindly insisted on my retaining the lead, and the only difference to me has been that they were more indulgent and more kind. I will not trespass on the rule of the evening by making any further political allusion, but I hope you will allow me to think that I was justified in making these remarks.

Unfortunately the Lord Provost has touched on a subject, with great kindness and even minuteness, which is one I cannot even allude to. I think that an author who speaks about his own books is almost as bad as a mother who talks about her own children. You know what happens under those circumstances. Everybody present soon gets wrapt in abstraction—one looks at the ceiling, another at the fire, one sighs, and another, perhaps, yawns. That is the general result of the introduction of such a topic, and I have always thought that a literary man who talks of his own writings must be put in the same category of boredom as the mother who dilates on the qualities of her darlings. Allow me now to express my surprise and delight that a rhapsody in 'Vivian Grey,' written nearly fifty years ago, has received the high honour, in one of the greatest cities of the kingdom, of being introduced to your indulgence. Gentlemen, on this subject I will merely say that, whatever the merits or demerits of my works, they were at least the result of my own feelings and my own observation.

Gentlemen, it is my fate, unfortunately, to pay a visit to one of the greatest commercial communities, I may say of the world, at a time when the commercial world is a little agitated. I have always found in my own experience that when the Bank rate of interest was at a minimum of 9 per cent., or something of that kind, my correspondence with Glasgow immensely increased. Therefore, I will make one or two remarks on that subject, because I must say that I cannot myself give my adhesion to the alarm which some feel at what some think a collapse in our commercial prosperity. I cannot myself see any signs of such declension; and I would rather attribute the somewhat startling results which have been recently witnessed to other causes.

I do not observe myself that there are any symptoms in Britain of reckless speculation, or any circumstances which can justify the alarm which has lately prevailed and the inconveniences which no doubt have been very generally felt. I see that there is no reduction in the returns of the railways or the wages of those connected with them, and I have always found that a very good sign as to the national prosperity and the general state of trade. I do not find that there are any dangerous commitments to foreign loans, which are generally so abundant, but less at this moment than usual, nor do I see any evidence of reckless speculation of any kind.

No doubt our young relations on the other side of the Atlantic—with that ardour which is characteristic of youth—have been doing some things somewhat improvident; no doubt they have commenced many undertakings without any capital whatever. We may perhaps attribute this outburst of speculation to the unexpected receipt of the 'Alabama' money. I have known young people, when they came into a fortune unexpectedly, playing rigs of that kind, and quite astonished at what it ends in. But the commercial system of this country is now so vast and various that, with the greatest respect for our Transatlantic cousins—and no one has a greater respect and regard for them than myself—I do not believe that the disorders which have arisen there could have occasioned, or were adequate to occasion, the disorders that have occurred in our own country with reference to the value of money. I attribute them to quite another cause, and if I touch on that cause, which I shall very briefly, I do it because I think the cause is not exhausted, and is deserving the grave attention of men who are so deeply interested in the prosperity of the country and the action of commerce as those I have the pleasure of meeting to-day.

I attribute the great monetary disturbance that has occurred, and is now to a certain degree acting very injuriously to trade—I attribute it to the great changes which the Governments in Europe are making with reference to their standard of value. You, of course, are perfectly acquainted with all these circumstances to which I allude. I attribute the present state of affairs very much to a Commission that was sitting in Paris at the time of the great Exhibition. That was a Commission the object of which was to establish a uniform coinage throughout the world—a beautiful idea of cosmopolitan philanthropy, which probably if it could be fulfilled would do no great harm; though I think it would be difficult to attain. The Commission of Paris never came to a definite recommendation on this subject, but they did on another subject, and that was that no time should be lost by any of the States of Europe in taking steps to establish a uniform gold standard of value. This, I know myself, arose from an opinion extremely prevalent among the statesmen of Europe and among distinguished economists and merchants abroad, that the commercial prosperity and preponderance of England were to be attributed to her gold standard. Now, our gold standard is, I think, an invaluable arrangement. I think that any country which has a gold standard of value should, to use a celebrated expression, think once, twice, and thrice before it gives it up. But it is the greatest delusion in the world to attribute the commercial preponderance and prosperity of England to our having a gold standard. Our gold standard is not the cause of our commercial prosperity, but the consequence of our commercial prosperity; and it is very well for us to have it: but you cannot establish a gold standard by violent means. It must arise gradually from the large transactions of the country, and the consequent command it may have over the precious metals. When the various States of Europe suddenly determined to have a gold standard, and took steps to carry it into effect, it was quite evident we must prepare ourselves for convulsions in the money-market, not occasioned by speculation or any old cause, which has been alleged, but by a new cause with which we are not yet sufficiently acquainted, and the consequences of which are very embarrassing; and that is the reason I have taken the opportunity of calling your attention to it.

Take the case of Germany. At this moment it is most remarkable, when there has been such a want of a gold standard in various parts of Europe, and even in England, where the strain has been so great, Germany has at this moment fifty millions sterling of gold coin virtually locked up; and it is locked up because it is the object of Germany to substitute a gold coinage for a silver coinage. While it has fifty millions value in gold coinage locked up, it has eighty or ninety millions of silver circulating, and they know very well, if they were to attempt to substitute violently the gold for the silver coinage—fifty millions of gold against ninety millions of silver—the consequence would be that the silver, already reduced in value, would become reduced still more, and the fifty millions of gold would all leave Germany. The consequence is that Germany is taking violent steps to get rid of this silver. The other day Germany sent a large amount of silver to Calcutta, and Germany could only by artificial means transmit it. The result was for a considerable time you could not buy a single bill on England. These are all circumstances calculated to disturb the course of commerce and manufacturing arrangements.

Then, again, take the case of France and America, which are floating on inconvertible paper; but France has also at this moment ninety millions sterling in silver coin. What must be the position of France with all her silver already depreciated, if Germany, to establish a gold standard, forces her own silver into France? France would be in a position of much embarrassment, and would make violent efforts to establish as soon as she can a gold coinage at any cost. Vast disturbance and fluctuations must arise from such circumstances. I regret to treat matters of this kind at a moment like this, because they require to be treated with more precision of language and with greater patience than either I or you can afford at this moment, but it did appear to me a subject to which I ought to call your attention.

You are commercial men, interested in the monetary system of the world; you ought to have your eye carefully upon the efforts which are making to establish a gold standard of value in Germany, in France, and, soon you will find, also in America. Legally, of course, there is a gold standard in America, but virtually there is not. Holland and all the Scandinavian States have also established a gold standard, probably to protect themselves from a depreciated currency; and when countries inundated with silver are trying to get rid of it, convulsions must come, and no one would be able to form an adequate idea of the monetary arrangements of the times in which he lives if he omits from his consideration the circumstances to which I have called your attention. I have drawn your attention to it to-day because you must know it is very difficult for me to address you under the conditions in which we meet. Munificent as is your hospitality, and cordial as may be your reception, it would scarcely do that our meeting to-day should be a mere interchange of compliments. To a certain degree that is very agreeable; one glass of liqueur is appropriate, but none of you would like to dine off a bottle of maraschino. A famous monarch, King Louis-Philippe, once said to me that he attributed the great success of the British nation in political life to their talking politics after dinner. Gentlemen, unfortunately to-day that is the only subject on which I may not enter, and therefore I hope that will be some excuse if I have touched on a question which is not a party question.

Let me, however, before I sit down, thank you, with my utmost heart, for the most cordial manner in which you have received me in your great city. I assure you the events of this day, both in the morning and evening, will not be easily erased from my memory. It is my first visit to your city. I think it is nearly half a century since I first visited Scotland. I remember it well, not only because I saw for the first time a memorable country, but because I made the personal acquaintance and became the guest of one of the best and greatest of men, the Lord of Abbotsford. He was a friend of my father, and he received me with that kindness which the illustrious do not, unfortunately, always bestow on the young. I remember walking with him in those new plantations of which he was so proud, by the banks of that River Tweed which he loved so well. He poured out all the treasures of his fancy and his memory, all the fire and music of his mind; he took as much pains to interest and entertain me as if, instead of being an unknown youth, I had been the Lord Rector of a famous University. That was the good nature of the man, which was as great as his genius.

How much has happened in those fifty years—a period more remarkable than any, I will venture to say, in the annals of mankind? I am not thinking of the rise and fall of empires, the change of dynasties, the establishment of governments. I am thinking of those revolutions of science, which have had much more effect than any political causes; which have changed the position and prospects of mankind more than all the conquests and all the codes, of all the Conquerors and all the Legislators that ever existed. In that time, gentlemen, you and your society have not been idle. You have raised your town to a position among the great cities of the world. Long may you retain that position; long may you retain that energy which has rendered your Clyde as famous as the Thames and the Seine; long may your factories be full of creative life; long may you appropriate the metallic treasures of your teeming soil; long may your docks and harbours receive and furnish navies. Under Divine Providence that prosperity will remain if you retain your public spirit. That depends upon your patriotism and your self-respect, and those sentiments can never in the British isles assume a more legitimate and fairer form than when they take the shape of loyalty and freedom. Gentlemen, I drink to your healths—all.

SPEECH ON RECEIVING THE FREEDOM OF THE CITY OF GLASGOW, IN A GOLD BOX, NOV. 20, 1873, *IN THE CITY HALL.*

MR. DISRAELI, who was received with loud and prolonged cheering, said—

MY LORD PROVOST AND GENTLEMEN,—Notwithstanding the kind and considerate terms in which the Lord Provost has alluded to the public accidents of my life, whether political or literary, and notwithstanding the cordial manner in which you have received those observations, I cannot for a moment permit any feeling of personal vanity to misinterpret the cause why I have received to-day this distinguished honour, bestowed in a manner which I cannot forget. I feel that it is owing to my connection with the University of Glasgow. I feel that you, the citizens of Glasgow, have, wisely and well, taken the opportunity of expressing the entire sympathy which subsists between the city and the University, and that you could do it in no manner more agreeable to them at this moment, and more convenient, than in honouring the individual whom they have so much honoured.

Gentlemen, I look upon that connection between the city and the University of Glasgow as a most valuable one, and which should be ever cherished. There is not any city connected with a University which has not become illustrious. The mutual influence of both institutions is most beneficial. On the one hand, it softens the habits of those who are devoted to the busy purposes of life; while the contiguity of the University to a great city like Glasgow infuses a knowledge of the world which those who are secluded in cloisters cannot command. I am happy to remember that this connection of affection between these two great institutions has always prevailed. I have read, at least certainly in works of the last century, that there existed in this city an example of a commercial and literary association, which may, perhaps, even now survive, which was illustrious from its members, and in which the merchants of Glasgow met names not second to any in the roll of British worthies. Adam Smith, known to the whole world as the highest authority on one of the highest of subjects, celebrated men of science, philosophers like the ingenious Reid and the illustrious Hutchinson, were members of that association, and exercised their influence upon the public mind and spirit of this community. Nor need

I remind you that the connection with the University has not been wanting in material advantage to this great city. The discoveries of philosophers in the University have influenced most advantageously the material fortunes of Glasgow. I need not allude to the inventions of Black and others which you have carried into practice, and which have given such an impetus to your industrial life, but I may perhaps be permitted to say, as Lord Rector of the University, that it would be most delightful to me if I could hear of some public acknowledgment on the part of some distinguished citizen of Glasgow on that subject, so that I might see the hall of our University raised with becoming splendour from the ground which is, unfortunately, now unoccupied.

I have observed that it is characteristic, a happy characteristic, of the age in which we live that men become their own executors, and I should be delighted to hear of some munificent endowment which would place our University in the position which it deserves. I feel confidence in appealing to the wealthy citizens of this opulent city, because it is, after all, in cities that enlightenment looks for its natural home; it is here, it is in great cities, especially those that have been intellectually influenced by the existence of Universities, that we find letters and arts and science flourish. The city, indeed, is the natural home of civilization It is in cities that have been discovered those inventions which have given an impulse to the education of the human mind. Priests and princes may have devised hieroglyphics and cuneiform writing, but nobody will deny that the alphabet was invented by merchants and manufacturers. Therefore, gentlemen, I trust that my election to the great office to which I have been raised may not be any impediment to the natural flow of the dispositions of the citizens of Glasgow, and that during the period that I may exercise any influence over the conduct of the University it will not be recorded as one in which it made no advance in its material fortunes.

Now, my Lord Provost and gentlemen, let me offer you my thanks for the distinction which you have conferred on me to-day. There is nothing which animates public men more than the prospect that they may obtain the sympathy and respect of their fellow citizens It is acts like these and scenes like these that sustain men in the turmoil and struggle of public life. Here we meet that approbation which is the great meed of public efforts; to live in the affections and afterwards in the memory of our fellow subjects is what every man looks to as the chief object of his career. I shall not forget the new position which I have occupied this day. I shall show at all times, not only that I am proud of the distinction which you have conferred upon me, but that I am faithful to the duties which it entails, and if ever the rights and interests of the city of Glasgow are invaded or imperilled there will be at least, I assure you, one Burgess on whose efforts to maintain them you need not fail to rely.

*REPLY TO THE ADDRESS OF THE SHORT TIME
COMMITTEE OF SCOTCH OPERATIVES, NOV.
23, 1873.*

MR. DISRAELI said—

GENTLEMEN,—I remember my support of the Ten Hours Bill as one of the most satisfactory incidents of my life, and therefore I need not say that I sympathize generally with your views. That measure was opposed by persons of great influence and by many parties in the State, and at one time it seemed impossible that it could have succeeded, because then neither of the two great parties avowedly upheld it. But as time advanced it was successful in its progress, and I am glad to say that those with whom I act generally in public life uniformly and unanimously upheld it; and they have been repaid for the great effort which they made—because it was not made without sacrifice—by the results. It has tended to the elevation of the working classes of this country. That elevation depends upon two causes. If their wages rise and their hours of labour diminish they are placed in a most favourable position; and if they do not avail themselves of the position they only prove that they are unworthy of it.

With regard to the first point, involving financial considerations—I refer to wages—no legislation can interfere. The rate of wages must be left to those inexorable rules of political economy to which we must all bow. They depend on demand and supply; but when you come to the hours of labour you then enter into social considerations, and in these the Legislature can interfere, and, if we use discretion and wisdom, no doubt to the advantage of the country and the working classes.

With regard to the particular point brought before me, it is not for the first time. Two years ago, in the centre of British industry, the great county of Lancaster, the glory of England, I received many communications and many deputations on the subject. I said at that time that it was unnecessary for me to state that I was favourable to the general policy, but as regarded the details of their particular proposal I requested that I should have confidence placed in me by the working classes; that they would allow me to consider its details when brought before Parliament in the shape of a practical measure, and that I could not pledge myself beyond a general sympathy with their cause. Since that time I have omitted no opportunity of making myself acquainted with the details of the subject brought before me to-day. I have communicated with great employers of labour. I have received from them much information, and I have made myself acquainted with their views, and all I can say now is that the result of my deliberations and of my researches is favourable to the views which you uphold; but I reserve to myself the right, for your interests as much as my own, to take care that whenever this subject is discussed I should be considered perfectly free.

I should be opposed to any change in which the general sympathies of the employers were not with the employed. I believe, myself, that with dispassionate discussion, and with those inquiries proceeding in an impartial spirit to which I have referred, the result would be that there would be very little difference of opinion between the working classes generally and their employers; but I should desire that in making any alterations of this kind there should be a general concurrence of sentiment. I only wish to make one reference to an observation made by one member of this deputation, that I should subserve the interests of the Conservative party by carrying out the views which you have expressed. That member of the deputation may rest assured that in upholding these views I am not guided by the interests of any party. My views on this subject were formed long before I was in the responsible position I have the honour to hold as the leader of a party. My opinions have never changed. And it is to me a subject of gratification that the large majority of those with whom I act in public life have the same opinion on this subject as myself. But I could not for a moment consider this question with reference to the interest of a political party.

I believe it is for the welfare of the country that the working classes should rise, as I think they are rising, in social and political consideration. I have confidence in the working classes. I do not know any other order of men which is so interested in maintaining the glory and greatness of this country. I have long been of opinion that if that state of things is brought about which seems fast approaching, when, with the increased remuneration for their toil which they now possess, they have reasonable diminution of their labour, nobody will be placed in a more happy position than the intelligent and educated working classes of this country.

It is only by labour and constant employment that life really is endurable. It is delightful with constant occupation—without it, it is intolerable. Your life is a life of happiness so long as your labour is not so excessive that you cannot cultivate your intelligence, while you enjoy those recreations of existence which the working classes to a great degree at present enjoy, and which fifty years ago they did not possess. In answer to your address to-day, I do not wish to pledge myself in any detail to what you request, but I am sure your own reflection will convince you from my past conduct that when the subject is brought before the Legislature, I shall take that course which I think best for the interests of the country and for your advantage.

SPEECH, IN THE CITY HALL, ON RECEIVING AN ADDRESS OF CONFIDENCE FROM THE CONSERVATIVE ASSOCIATION OF GLASGOW, NOVEMBER 22, 1873.

Mr. DISRAELI, on rising to address the meeting, was received with the most enthusiastic cheers. He said—

MR. CHAIRMAN AND GENTLEMEN,—I am not using merely conventional language when I express to you the high honour that I feel in receiving this address from the Conservative Association of Glasgow. The gratification is increased by the chair being filled this day by one who was formerly a colleague of mine in Parliament, and whom, with others around me, I learnt to respect, and more than respect, for he gained the heart of the House of Commons while he sat there.

Gentlemen, I will not conceal from you, and, indeed, many and most of you know it, that when it was first suggested to me to receive this distinction, and to meet you here, after great reflection, I felt it my duty—though with pain—to refuse the honour which was intended for me. I did so, because I thought that, upon the whole, as my visit to Glasgow was an academic and neutral visit, it would be better that nothing should occur that might in any way make an exception to that general sentiment of respect which it is my pride and pleasure to say I have received from all classes and all parties in this city. And I must take this opportunity, as it may be the last I shall have, without reference to any political opinions, of expressing to the citizens of Glasgow my lively sense of the kind and considerate manner in which they have received me, and I must say the too great indulgence even of those who do not generally agree with me in political opinion.

But, Gentlemen, when I had been here some little time it was represented to me by those who spoke for a large body of my fellow countrymen that it seemed very hard upon them who, from their pursuits and other reasons, could take no part in august academical functions, or in the splendour of civic banquets, that, feeling deeply as they did on political subjects, one whom, however unworthy he may be of their confidence, they still regard as their chief, should be resident for nearly a week in this great city, in communication, apparently, with all but his humbler friends, who perhaps looked on him with not less confidence and affection. And I confess to you that although it had been my original hope that not a word should have fallen from these lips during my visit to Glasgow which should have been discordant to any individual in the city, I could not resist this appeal. It did appear to me to be so unfair, I would say so unkind and ungenerous, that I assented, after due consideration, to receive this address and meet you as we meet to-day, on terms which will permit me to make some observations to you on the present state of public affairs.

And I will here say, that there may be no misunderstanding with reference to some paragraphs I have seen in the public papers, that I never was asked and never assented to meet any separate body particularly styled 'Conservative Working Men.' I have never been myself at all favourable to a system which would induce Conservatives who are working men to form societies confined merely to their class. In the church and at the polling-booth all are equal. All that concerns Conservative working men and interests them concerns and interests the great body of Conservatives of whom they form a portion. Therefore, it is to the Conservative Association I see before me, of whom a very considerable majority consists of working men —it is to that Association that I address myself.

Mr. Chairman and Gentlemen,—I believe I may describe the position of this country as one of great prosperity. There is no doubt that during the last three years that prosperity has been generally acknowledged. There are some who suppose that it may have now received a check. If it has received a check it will increase, I hope, our circumspection, but I must express my own opinion that no substantial diminution in the sources of the prosperity so apparent during the last three years has occurred. I think we may fairly say the state of this country is one of great prosperity, and although I believe and know that it is a prosperity for which we are not indebted either to Whigs or Tories, although I know that it has been occasioned in a considerable degree, under Providence, by fortuitous though felicitous circumstances, I am perfectly ready, speaking to-day, as I hope to speak, in the fairest terms on public affairs, which I believe to be quite consistent with the position of the leader of a party—I am ready to give to Her Majesty's Government credit for the prosperity we feel and acknowledge.

With regard to Her Majesty's Ministers themselves, I will be equally candid, equally fair—I will take them at their own estimate. They have lost few opportunities of informing the country that they are men distinguished for commanding talent, admirable eloquence and transcendent administrative abilities. I dispute none of these propositions any more than I do the prosperity of the country. They also tell us that the country being so prosperous, and they having all these personal advantages, they have taken the opportunity during the last few years of passing measures of immense magnitude, only equalled by the benefit they have conferred upon the people.

Now, gentlemen, I will not question their own estimate of their ability, or even for a moment their own description of their achievements; but I ask this question,—What is the reason, when the country is so prosperous, when its affairs are administered by so gifted a Government, and when they have succeeded during five years in passing measures so vast and beneficent—what is the reason that Her Majesty's Ministers are going about regretting that they are so unpopular? Now, gentlemen, I beg you to observe that I did not say Her Majesty's Ministers are unpopular. It is they who say so. I stated their own case and their own position; I say that, under the circumstances I have put fairly before you, it is a remarkable circumstance, and the question must be inquired into—why persons in the position of Her Majesty's Government should on every occasion deplore the unpopularity they have incurred.

Now my opinion, gentlemen, is that that is not a question of mere curiosity—it is one that, as I think I shall show you, concerns the honour and the interests of the country. If the country is so prosperous—if Her Majesty's Ministers are so gifted— if they have had such an ample opportunity of showing the talents which they possess—if they have done all this good—if they have availed themselves of this signal opportunity to effect such great results, then the only inference we can draw from the unpopularity which they themselves deplore is that the people of this country is a fickle and ungrateful people. Therefore it is not a question of mere curiosity. It is a question that ought to be answered.

If there be those who suppose that the people of this country, as I hold, is not a fickle or ungrateful people—that they are a people who may be mistaken—that may be misled, but that they are a people who, on the whole, are steadfast in their convictions, and especially in their political convictions, then this question, if left unanswered, as Her Majesty's Ministers have placed the circumstances before the country, is a slur on the character of the people of this kingdom. I say it ought to be answered; and a short time since—some two months ago—I answered it.

It appeared to me, at that moment especially, when Her Majesty's Government, by their ablest and most powerful representatives, were deploring their unpopularity, and asking the reason why, or rather intimating by inference that it was the fault of the people, not of the Government, that some one should give an answer to that question. I gave it, and in a very brief form—in the most condensed and the most severely accurate form. There is not an expression in that description of the conduct of the Government which was not well weighed; there is not a word for which I had not warranty, and for which I could not adduce testimony ample and abounding. There was only one characteristic of that description which was not noticed at the time, and which I will now confess—it was not original, for six months before, in the House of Commons, I had used the same expressions and made the same statement—not in a hole or corner, but on the most memorable night of the Session, when there were six hundred members of the House of Commons present, when on the debate then taking place avowedly the fate of the Ministry depended.

It was at midnight that I rose to speak, and made the statement almost similar in expression, though perhaps stronger and more lengthened than the one which has become the cause of recent controversy. The Prime Minister followed me in that debate. The House of Commons knew what was depending upon the verdict about to be taken, and with all that knowledge they came to a division, and by a majority terminated the existence of the Government. Gentlemen, it surprises me, then, that having repeated that statement six months after, with the advantage of six months' more experience and observation, it should have so much offended Her Majesty's Government. The Ministers sighed and their newspapers screamed. The question I have to ask, and in this your interests are vitally concerned—the question is, was the statement I made a true and accurate one? You cannot answer statements of this kind by saying 'Oh, fie! how very rude.' You must at least adduce arguments in order to prove that the statement which you do not sanction is one that ought not to have been made. And therefore I ask you to-day, in the first place, is it or is it not true that the Irish Church has been despoiled? Is it or is it not true that the gentlemen of Ireland have been severely amerced? Is it or is it not true that a Royal Commission has been issued which has dealt with the ancient endowments of this country in so ruthless a manner that Parliament has frequently been called upon to interfere, and has addressed the Crown to arrest their propositions? Are these facts or are they not?

Well, I did then venture to say that the Ministers had 'harassed trades and worried professions,' as reasons why men naturally become unpopular. Was that true or was it not? Because, after all, everything depends on the facts of the statement. I will not enter into a long catalogue of trades, commencing with the important trade of which we have heard so much, and which has made itself felt at so many elections, down to the humblest trade—the lucifer match makers who fell upon their knees in Palace-yard. I suppose there are some Scotch farmers present, or, at least, those who are intimately connected with them. I want to know whether their trade was harassed when a proposition was brought before the House of Commons to tax their carts and horses, and all the machinery of their cultivation? I know how the proposition was received in England, and I doubt not the Scotch farmers, like the English, felt extremely harassed by it. I want to know what is the reason why there is this crusade throughout the country against Schedule D of the Income Tax. The Income Tax has been borne for 30 years with great self-sacrifice, and endured with great loyalty by the people of this country. It is at this moment at the lowest pitch it ever reached; how is it, then, that it is at this moment more unpopular than it was at any time during the long period we endured it, and at a much higher figure? It is on account of the assessment of the trades of England under that schedule. It is the vexatious and severe assessment that has harassed all trades under that Act, who are not particularly pleased when, after paying five quarters of Income Tax in one year, they learn also that they are in arrears.

Then, have the professions been worried? Is it not true that at this moment a Royal Commission is examining in London into the grievances of six thousand officers? Ask the Naval profession whether they have not been worried. During the course of the present Government the whole administrative system of the Admiralty, the Council that had always a wise and vast influence in the management of the Navy, and the peculiar and important office of the Secretary, were all swept away; and in spite, I may say, of the nightly warnings of a right hon. friend of mine now lost to us all and his country, the ablest Minister of the Admiralty during the present reign—notwithstanding his nightly warnings that they were so conducting the administration of the Navy that they would probably fall into some disaster. His remonstrances were in vain, and it was not till the most costly vessel of the State foundered, and the perilous voyage of the 'Megæra' had been made, that the country resolved to stand it no longer, they rescinded the whole of this worrying arrangement, and appointed a new First Lord to re-establish the old system. Is that worrying a profession, or is it not?

Well, gentlemen, I can speak of another profession —a profession not the least considerable in the State— the Civil Service profession. Has it been worried or is it now in a process of worrying, or is it not? There are many even in this room well acquainted with the Civil Service in all its departments. Let them decide. I might say the same of the legal profession, for I have heard the lawyers on both sides of the House in the debates of last Session agree in imploring the Government not to continue propositions which would infallibly weaken the administration of justice in this country. But with professions and trades it is not merely those directly attacked, but it is every one that is harassed and worried, because no one knows whose turn will come next.

Well, I did say to the House of Commons, and I afterwards expressed it in another form—I said the Ministers had attacked every class and institution, from the highest to the lowest in the country. Is that true or is it not? Is it not a fact that Her Majesty's Government on every occasion of which they could avail themselves during the last three years attacked the House of Lords—scoffed at the existence of its high functions, and even defied its decisions, until the result proved that the House of Lords was extremely popular in the country, and Her Majesty's Government were obliged themselves to confess that they were exceedingly unpopular. But you must also remember this,—that the same body of men who thus attacked the House of Lords also brought in a bill which attacked the poor inheritance of the widow and the orphan.

Now, I think I have shown that from the highest to the lowest the same system prevailed. What occurred in the interval? The Churches of England and Scotland have been threatened. It has been publicly stated by the highest authority in the House of Commons that he did not believe that the present House of Commons would sanction the views of those who wished to pull down these venerable establishments, but he recommended them to agitate out of doors and endeavour to excite public opinion against them.

Then, again, I said jobs were perpetrated that outraged public opinion. Is that true, or is it not? Is it not the fact that two years ago public opinion was outraged by persons being appointed to important offices in Church and State in direct violation of the language of Acts of Parliament?—that a dispensing power in that respect was exercised by the Minister, that dispensing power which forfeited the crown of James II. Was not public indignation roused to the highest pitch upon the Collier appointment? Were these acts perpetrated or not, and did they outrage public opinion? Every one knows that public opinion was outraged.

I have said, also, that they stumbled into errors which were always discreditable and sometimes ruinous. That was called violent language. Gentlemen, I never use violent language. Violent language is generally weak language; but I hope my language is sometimes strong. Now, let us look at this statement. I said that they stumbled into errors which were always discreditable and sometimes ruinous? Was the Zanzibar contract an 'error,' and was it not 'discreditable?' Was the conduct of the Treasury in allowing a subordinate officer to misappropriate nearly a million of the public money an 'error,' and was it not 'discreditable?' When the Government had referred the Alabama Claims to the arbitrament of a third State, was not the change of the Law of Nations by the Three Rules an 'error,' and was that not 'discreditable?' And besides being 'discreditable,' was it not ruinous?

Now, I have given an answer to the question why the Government, with transcendent abilities, as they tell us, with magnificent exploits which they are always extolling, and with a country whose prosperity is so palpable, are unpopular. I tell them why. They have harassed and worried the country, and there was no necessity for any of the acts they have committed. I have put it in condensed and, I am sure, accurate language. There was a celebrated writer, one of the greatest masters of our language, who wrote the history of the last four years of the reign of Queen Anne, which was the duration of an illustrious Ministry. I have written the history of a Ministry that has lasted five years, and I have immortalized the spirit of their policy in five lines.

And now, gentlemen, I will tell you what is the unfortunate cause of this political embarrassment. Why, with such favourable circumstances as the present Government have experienced; why with the great ability which no man is more aware that they possess than myself; why, with the most anxious and earnest desire for which I give them entire credit to do their duty to their Sovereign and their fellow countrymen, the result has been so mortifying. I told it two years ago to the assembled county of Lancaster, when I met not only the greatest proprietors of its soil, but deputations and delegations of its choicest citizens from every town and city of that great county. I told them, speaking with the sense of the deepest responsibility, which I trust also animates me now—I told them that the cause was, that this Government, unfortunately, in its beginning had been founded on a principle of violence, and that fatal principle had necessarily vitiated their whole course.

And what have we gained by that principle of violence? Let us consider it, here even, with impartiality and perfect candour. I am now referring to the Irish policy of the Ministry. I say it is quite possible for public men, with the view of obtaining some great object advantageous to the country, to devise and pass measures which may utterly fail in accomplishing their purpose; and yet, however mortifying to themselves, however disappointing to the country, there would be no stain upon their reputation. We cannot command, but we must endeavour in public life to deserve, success. If, therefore, it is said that the Government proposed the large measures which they did with respect to Ireland in order to terminate the grievances of years and the embarrassment to England—which the state of Ireland certainly was—although they may have failed, their position was one which still might be a position of respect. That they have failed in this instance no one can doubt. A great portion of Ireland at this moment is in a state of veiled rebellion.

But what I charge upon the Government is this, not that their measures have failed—for all measures may fail —not that their measures failed to prevent or to suppress this veiled rebellion in Ireland, but that the measures, which they brought forward to appease and settle, to tranquillize and consolidate Ireland, are the very cause that this veiled rebellion has occurred.

For, gentlemen, what was the principle upon which the whole of their policy with respect to Ireland was founded? What was the principle upon which they induced Parliament to confiscate and to despoil the Church and private property in Ireland? It was that Ireland must be governed on Irish principles—the administration of Ireland must be carried on with reference to Irish feeling. If that is a sound principle and a sound sentiment in politics, it is a perfect vindication of what is occurring in the city of Dublin at this moment—viz. an assembly of men whose avowed object is to dissever the connection between the two countries. If we are not to legislate for Ireland with reference to Imperial feelings and general and national interests—if we are only to legislate with reference to Irish feelings, it is perfectly evident that if a majority of the Irish people take any idea in the world into their heads, however ruinous to themselves, and however fatal to the Empire, that policy must be recognized by this country. It is, therefore, to the principle avowedly, ostentatiously, brought forward by the Ministry as the basis of their Irish policy that I trace the dangerous condition in which Ireland is placed. Well, then, I say this policy of violence, for which such sacrifices were made, for which institutions and interests which were at least faithful to Britain were sacrificed—this policy of violence has led only to a state of affairs, unfortunately, more unsatisfactory than that which prevailed before.

Now, gentlemen, I observe in the papers that the day is fixed for the re-assembling of Parliament. The time is not yet very near, but when you find Her Majesty has appointed the day for our re-assembling, it is an intimation that we must begin to consider the public business a little, and, therefore, it is not altogether inconvenient that we should be talking upon these matters to-day. Now, when we meet Parliament I apprehend the first business that will be brought before us will be the Ashantee war. Upon that subject my mouth is closed. I will not even make an observation upon the railway, which I believe has been returned to England. Whenever this intention of the Government, probably, to consider the question, Her Majesty's Government may at this moment be considering the question of further Parliamentary Reform.

Now, there are two points which the Government ought to consider when they come to that question. The first is the expediency of having any further Parliamentary Reform. They will have to remember that very wise statesmen have been of opinion that there is no more dangerous and feebler characteristic of a State than perpetually to be dwelling on what is called organic change. The habit, it has been said in politics, of perpetually considering your political constitution can only be compared to that of the individual who is always considering the state of his health and his physical constitution. You know what occurs in such circumstances—he becomes infirm and valetudinarian. In fact, there is a school of politics which looks at the English Constitution as valetudinarian. They are always looking at its tongue and feeling its pulse, and devising means by which they may give it a tonic. The Government will have to consider that very important point, first of all, whether it is expedient. I am not giving any opinion upon it—being only a private member of Parliament that is quite unnecessary—but I am indicating that the consideration would occur to a responsible statesman. They will also have to consider this important point, that whatever Minister embarks in a campaign of Parliamentary Reform must make up his mind that he will necessarily arrest the progress of all other public business in the country.

I will show you to what extent that consideration should prevail. Parliamentary Reform, as a new question, was introduced in the House of Commons in 1852 by Lord John Russell, and from 1852 to 1866 or the end of 1865 it was introduced annually; four Prime Ministers had pledged themselves to the expediency of Parliamentary Reform; the subject made no progress in Parliament, but took up a great deal of time; a great portion of the Parliamentary Sessions for these twelve or thirteen years was taken up by discussions on Parliamentary Reform; and the country got very ill-tempered, finding that no reform was ever advanced, and other and more important subjects were neglected. At last it was taken up by men determined to carry it: first by Lord Russell, who did not carry it, and afterwards by others; but observe, the whole of 1866, 1867, and 1868 were entirely absorbed by the subject of Parliamentary Reform. Therefore, you will observe that when important subjects in legislation are pressing, you must be prepared to discourage any further demand for Parliamentary Reform unless you feel an insuperable necessity for it, because if you want Parliamentary Reform you cannot have any of those large measures with regard to local taxation or other subjects in which you are all so much interested. That is the first consideration for the Government of the present day to determine, whether they shall embark in the question of Parliamentary Reform. Is it necessary? Is the necessity of such a character that it outweighs the immense inconvenience of sacrificing all other public and progressive measures for the advancement of this particular measure?

Then there comes another subject of consideration. I dwell upon these matters because I apprehend that one of the reasons of our meeting this evening is that upon questions which are likely to engage the public attention so far as those whom you honour with your confidence can give you any guidance, it is as well that I should indicate to you briefly my general views of the situation. Now, the next point, therefore, that Government will have to consider if they make up their minds to bring forward a measure of Parliamentary Reform is the character of the measure, and that will be a most anxious question for them to decide.

I think I may say without conceit that the subject of Parliamentary reform is one that I am entitled to speak upon at least with some degree of authority. I have given to it the consideration of some forty years, and am responsible for the most important measure on the subject that has been carried. I would say this, that it is impossible to go further in the direction of Parliamentary Reform than the Bill of

1867-68 without entirely subverting the whole of the borough representation of this country. I do not mean to say that if there was a place disfranchised to-morrow for corruption it would not be possible to enfranchise a very good place in its stead; but, speaking generally, you cannot go beyond the Act of 1867 without making up your mind entirely to break up the borough representation of this country. The people of Great Britain ought to be aware that that is the necessary consequence.

So far as I am concerned I never could view the matter in a party light. If I were to accustom myself to view it in a party light I might look with unconcern on this difficulty, for the smaller boroughs of the country are not, on the whole, favourable to our views. I am proud to think our party is supported by the great counties, and now to a great extent by great towns and cities; but I do not consider the small boroughs favourable to Conservative views. It is the national sympathies and wide sentiments of those who live in our great cities that are much more calculated to rally round the cause in which we are deeply concerned—the greatness and glory of our country. This ought to be known, that if you really intend to have a further measure of Parliamentary Reform, and have digested that large meal which you had a few years ago, there is no borough in England with under forty thousand inhabitants that would have any claim to be represented even by one member. Now that is a very important consideration, if, as we are told, the small boroughs of between ten and thirty thousand inhabitants are the backbone of the Liberal party. They may be, and I think they are. But I should be very sorry to see them disfranchised. They are centres of public spirit and intelligence in the country, influencing much the districts in which they are situated, and affording a various representation of the mind and life of the country. But it is inevitable that should occur, and I think, therefore, it ought to be well understood by the country when you have persons, without the slightest consideration, saying they are prepared to vote for this, or who are all in favour of that, whereas they have not really mastered the question.

So far as I am concerned, any proposition to change the representation of the people brought forward by Her Majesty's Government will have my respectful and candid consideration. But I say at once that I will vote for no measure of that kind, or of that class that is brought forward by some irresponsible individual who wants, on the eve of a general election, to make a clap-trap career. I think it perfectly disgusting for individuals to jump up in the House of Commons, and without the slightest responsibility, official or moral, make propositions which demand the gravest consideration of prolonged and protracted

Cabinets, with all the responsibility attaching to experienced statesmen.

Now, gentlemen, although I have rather exceeded the time I had intended, there are one or two more remarks I should like to make on subjects which interest us all. And first, as the only feature in our domestic life that gives me uneasiness, are the relations at present between capital and labour, and between the employers and the employed—I must say one word upon that subject. If there are any relations in the world which should be those of sympathy and perfect confidence, they always appear to be the relations which should subsist between employers and employed, and especially in manufacturing life. They are, in fact, much more intimate and more necessary relations than those which subsist between landlords and tenants. It is an extremely painful thing that of late years we so frequently hear of misunderstandings between the employers and the employed—that they look upon each other with suspicion—with mutual suspicion—as if each were rapaciously inclined either to obtain or retain the greater share of the profits of their trade; those incidents with which you are all acquainted, of a very painful nature, being the consequence.

Now I am not talking of demands for an increase of wages when men are carrying on what is called a roaring trade—I believe that is the classical epithet. When a roaring trade is going on, I am not at all surprised that working men should ask for an increase of wages. But the trade sometimes ceases to roar, when wages naturally, on the same principle, assume a form more adapted to the circumstances. But, no doubt, during the last twenty years there appears to have been, not a passing and temporary cause of disturbance, like the incidents of trade being very active or reduced, but some permanent cause disturbing prices, which alike confuses the employer in his calculations as to profits and embarrasses the employed from the greater expenditure which they find it necessary to make.

Now, I cannot but feel myself—having given to the subject some consideration—I cannot help feeling that the large and continuous increase of the precious metals, especially during the last twenty years, has certainly produced no inconsiderable effect on prices.

I will not on an occasion like this enter into anything like an abstruse discussion. I confine myself to giving my opinion and the results; and this moral, which I think is worthy of consideration. If it can be shown accurately and scientifically that there is a cause affecting a prominent class, reducing the average remuneration of the employed, and confusing and confounding the employer in his calculations as to profits —if that can be shown, and if it is proved to be the result of inexorable laws, far beyond the reach of legislatures, and of circumstances over which human beings have no control—I think if that could be shown, and employers and employed had sufficient acuteness and knowledge—and I am sure that in Scotland there is no lack of both—it would very much change those mutual feelings of suspicion and sentiments of a not pleasant character which occasionally prevail when they find that they are both of them the victims, as it were, of some inexorable law of public economy which cannot be resisted. I think, instead of supposing that each wanted to take advantage of the other they would feel inclined to put their shoulders to the wheel, accurately ascertain whether this be true, and come to some understanding which would very much mitigate the relations which subsist between them. I have little doubt the effect would be to increase the average rate of wages, with my views as to the effect of the continuous increase of the precious metals. But, at the same time, I have not the slightest doubt the employer would, in the nature of things, find adequate compensation for the new position in which he would find himself.

There is one point, before I sit down, to which I wish to call your attention. Because, if I am correct in saying that the question of the relations between the employer and employed is the only one that gives me anxiety at home, there is a subject abroad to which I think I ought, on an occasion like this, to draw your

39 Paternoster Row, E.C.
London: *March* 1873.

GENERAL LIST OF WORKS

PUBLISHED BY

Messrs. LONGMANS, GREEN, READER, and DYER.

Arts, Manufactures, &c.	14	Miscellaneous Works and Popular Metaphysics	7
Astronomy, Meteorology, Popular Geography, &c.	8	Natural History & Popular Science	9
Biographical Works	4	Poetry and The Drama	19
Chemistry, Medicine, Surgery, and the Allied Sciences	11	Religious and Moral Works	15
Criticism, Philosophy, Polity, &c.	5	Rural Sports, &c.	19
Fine Arts and Illustrated Editions	13	Travels, Voyages, &c.	17
History, Politics, and Historical Memoirs	1	Works of Fiction	18
Index	21—24	Works of Utility and General Information	20

History, Politics, Historical Memoirs, &c.

Estimates of the English Kings from William the Conqueror to George III. By J. Langton Sanford, Author of 'Studies and Illustrations of the Great Rebellion' &c. Crown 8vo. price 12s. 6d.

The History of England from the Fall of Wolsey to the Defeat of the Spanish Armada. By James Anthony Froude, M.A.

Cabinet Edition, 12 vols. cr. 8vo. £3 12s.
Library Edition, 12 vols. 8vo. £8 18s.

The English in Ireland in the Eighteenth Century. By James Anthony Froude, M.A. late Fellow of Exeter College, Oxford. In Two Volumes. Vol. I., 8vo. price 16s.

The History of England from the Accession of James II. By Lord Macaulay:—

Student's Edition, 2 vols. crown 8vo. 12s.
People's Edition, 4 vols. crown 8vo. 16s.
Cabinet Edition, 8 vols. post 8vo. 48s.
Library Edition, 5 vols. 8vo. £4.

Lord Macaulay's Works. Complete and uniform Library Edition. Edited by his Sister, Lady Trevelyan. 8 vols. 8vo. with Portrait, price £5. 5s. cloth, or £8. 8s. bound in tree-calf by Rivère.

Memoirs of Baron Stockmar. By his Son, Baron E. von Stockmar. Translated from the German by G. A. M. Edited by Max Müller, M.A. 2 vols. crown 8vo. price 21s.

Varieties of Vice-Regal Life. By Major-General Sir William Denison, K.C.B. late Governor-General of the Australian Colonies, and Governor of Madras. With Two Maps. 2 vols. 8vo. 28s.

On Parliamentary Government in England: its Origin, Development, and Practical Operation. By Alpheus Todd, Librarian of the Legislative Assembly of Canada. 2 vols. 8vo. price £1. 17s.

The Constitutional History of England since the Accession of George III. 1760—1860. By Sir Thomas Erskine May, K.C.B. Cabinet Edition (the Third), thoroughly revised. 3 vols. crown 8vo. price 18s.

The History of England, from the Earliest Times to the Year 1865. By C. D. Yonge, Regius Professor of Modern History in Queen's College, Belfast. New Edition. Crown 8vo. 7s. 6d.

Lectures on the History of England, from the Earliest Times to the Death of King Edward II. By William Longman. With Maps and Illustrations. 8vo. 15s.

The History of the Life and Times of Edward the Third. By WILLIAM LONGMAN. With 9 Maps, 8 Plates, and 16 Woodcuts. 2 vols. 8vo. 28s.

History of Civilization in England and France, Spain and Scotland. By HENRY THOMAS BUCKLE. New Edition of the entire work, with a complete INDEX. 3 vols. crown 8vo. 24s.

Realities of Irish Life. By W. STEUART TRENCH, late Land Agent in Ireland to the Marquess of Lansdowne, the Marquess of Bath, and Lord Digby. Fifth Edition. Crown 8vo. 6s.

The Student's Manual of the History of Ireland. By M. F. CUSACK, Authoress of 'The Illustrated History of Ireland.' Crown 8vo. price 6s.

A Student's Manual of the History of India, from the Earliest Period to the Present. By Colonel MEADOWS TAYLOR, M.R.A.S. M.R.I.A. Second Thousand. Crown 8vo. with Maps, 7s. 6d.

The History of India, from the Earliest Period to the close of Lord Dalhousie's Administration. By JOHN CLARK MARSHMAN. 3 vols. crown 8vo. 22s. 6d.

Indian Polity; a View of the System of Administration in India. By Lieut.-Col. GEORGE CHESNEY. Second Edition, revised, with Map. 8vo. 21s.

A Colonist on the Colonial Question. By JEHU MATHEWS, of Toronto, Canada. Post 8vo. price 6s.

An Historical View of Literature and Art in Great Britain from the Accession of the House of Hanover to the Reign of Queen Victoria. By J. MURRAY GRAHAM, M.A. 8vo. price 12s.

Waterloo Lectures; a Study of the Campaign of 1815. By Colonel CHARLES C. CHESNEY, R.E. late Professor of Military Art and History in the Staff College. Second Edition. 8vo. with Map, 10s. 6d.

Memoir and Correspondence relating to Political Occurrences in June and July 1834. By EDWARD JOHN LITTLETON, First Lord Hatherton. Edited, from the Original Manuscript, by HENRY REEVE, C.B. D.C.L. 8vo. price 7s. 6d.

Chapters from French History; St. Louis, Joan of Arc, Henri IV. with Sketches of the Intermediate Periods. By J. H. GURNEY, M.A. New Edition. Fcp. 8vo. 6s. 6d.

Royal and Repub[lican] A Series of Essays [
'Edinburgh,' 'Quarterl[y] Foreign' Reviews. [
C.B. D.C.L. 2 vols. 8v[

The Imperial and [In]stitutions of the Britann[ic] Indian Institutions. CREASY, M.A. &c. W[i] price 15s.

The Oxford Reform[ers] Erasmus, and Thomas [
tory of their Fellow-W[ork] SEEBOHM. Second Edi[tion]

A History of Gree[ce] Original Authorities, and [
the use of Colleges and S[
GEORGE W. COX, M.[A] Trinity College, Oxfor[d] Aryan Mythology' &c.

The History of Gree[ce] WALL, D.D. Lord Bisl[
8 vols. fcp. 28s.

The Tale of the [Great] War, from the Histories [
GEORGE W. COX, M.[Trin. Coll. Oxon. Fcp.

The Sixth Orient[al Monarchy,] or, the Geography, His[
ties of Parthia. Collec[
from Ancient and Mo[
GEORGE RAWLINSON, [
fessor of Ancient Histor[y] of Oxford, and Canon of [
Maps and Illustrations.

Greek History from [Thucydides] to Alexander, in a Ser[
Plutarch. Revised and [
CLOUGH. Fcp. with 44 [

History of the R[omans under] the Empire. By Ver[y Rev.] MERIVALE, D.C.L. Dean [
8vo. price 48s.

The Fall of the [Roman Re]public; a Short Histor[y
tury of the Commonwe[alth.
Author. 12mo. 7s. 6d.

Encyclopædia of [
Historical and Biograp[hical,
the Dates of all the [
History, including T[
Wars, Battles, &c.; Inci[
of Eminent Men, Scien[
phical Discoveries, Mecl[
and Social, Domestic, ar[
provements. By B. B. [
and W. L. R. CATES. 8[

The History of Rome. By WILHELM IHNE. English Edition, translated and revised by the Author. VOLS. I. and II. 8vo. 30s.

History of European Morals from Augustus to Charlemagne. By W. E. H. LECKY, M.A. 2 vols. 8vo. price 28s.

History of the Rise and Influence of the Spirit of Rationalism in Europe. By the same Author. Cabinet Edition (the Fourth). 2 vols. crown 8vo. price 16s.

God in History; or, the Progress of Man's Faith in the Moral Order of the World. By the late Baron BUNSEN. Translated from the German by SUSANNA WINKWORTH; with a Preface by Dean STANLEY. 3 vols. 8vo. 42s.

Introduction to the Science of Religion: Four Lectures delivered at the Royal Institution of Great Britain in February and March 1870; with a Lecture on the Philosophy of Mythology and an Essay on False Analogies in Religion. By F. MAX MÜLLER, M.A., Professor of Comparative Philology at Oxford. [*In the Press.*

Socrates and the Socratic Schools. Translated from the German of Dr. E. ZELLER, with the Author's approval, by the Rev. OSWALD J. REICHEL, B.C.L. and M.A. Crown 8vo. 8s. 6d.

The Stoics, Epicureans, and Sceptics. Translated from the German of Dr. E. ZELLER, with the Author's approval, by OSWALD J. REICHEL, B.C.L. and M.A. Crown 8vo. 14s.

The English Reformation. By F. C. MASSINGBERD, M.A. late Chancellor of Lincoln. 4th Edition. Fcp. 8vo. 7s 6d.

Three Centuries of Modern History. By CHARLES DUKE YONGE, Regius Professor of Modern History and English Literature in Queen's College, Belfast. Crown 8vo. 7s. 6d.

Saint-Simon and Saint-Simonism; a Chapter in the History of Socialism in France. By ARTHUR J. BOOTH, M.A. Crown 8vo. price 7s. 6d.

The History of Philosophy, from Thales to Comte. By GEORGE HENRY LEWES. Fourth Edition, corrected and partly rewritten. 2 vols. 8vo. 32s.

The Mythology of the Aryan Nations. By GEORGE W. COX, M.A. late Scholar of Trinity College, Oxford. 2 vols. 8vo. price 28s.

Maunder's Historical Treasury; comprising a General Introductory Outline of Universal History, and a Series of Separate Histories. Fcp. 8vo. price 6s.

Critical and Historical Essays contributed to the *Edinburgh Review* by the Right Hon. Lord MACAULAY:—
STUDENT'S EDITION, crown 8vo, 6s.
PEOPLE'S EDITION, 2 vols. crown 8vo. 8s.
CABINET EDITION, 4 vols. 24s.
LIBRARY EDITION, 3 vols. 8vo. 36s.

History of the Early Church, from the First Preaching of the Gospel to the Council of Nicæa, A.D. 325. By the Author of 'Amy Herbert.' New Edition. Fcp. 8vo. 4s. 6d.

Sketch of the History of the Church of England to the Revolution of 1688. By the Right Rev. T. V. SHORT, D.D. Lord Bishop of St. Asaph. Eighth Edition. Crown 8vo. 7s. 6d.

Essays on the Rise and Progress of the Christian Religion in the West of Europe. From the Reign of Tiberius to the End of the Council of Trent. By JOHN EARL RUSSELL. 8vo. [*In the Press.*

History of the Christian Church, from the Ascension of Christ to the Conversion of Constantine. By E. BURTON, D.D. late Regius Prof. of Divinity in the University of Oxford. Fcp. 8vo. 3s. 6d.

History of the Christian Church, from the Death of St. John to the Middle of the Second Century; comprising a full Account of the Primitive Organisation of Church Government, and the Growth of Episcopacy. By T. W. MOSSMAN, B.A. Rector of East and Vicar of West Torrington, Lincolnshire. 8vo. price 16s.

Causality; or, the Philosophy of Law Investigated. By GEORGE JAMIESON, B.D. of Old Machar. Second Edition, greatly enlarged. 8vo. price 12s.

Speeches of the Right Hon. Lord MACAULAY, corrected by Himself. People's Edition, crown 8vo. 3s. 6d.

Lord Macaulay's Speeches on Parliamentary Reform in 1831 and 1832. 16mo. price ONE SHILLING.

A Dictionary of the English Language. By R. G. LATHAM, M.A. M.D. F.R.S. Founded on the Dictionary of Dr. S. JOHNSON, as edited by the Rev. H. J. TODD, with numerous Emendations and Additions. 4 vols. 4to. price £7.

Thesaurus of English Words and Phrases, classified and arranged so as to facilitate the expression of Ideas, and assist in Literary Composition. By P. M. ROGET, M.D. New Edition. Crown 8vo. 10s. 6d.

Three Centuries of English Lierature. By CHARLES DUKE YONGE, Regius Professor of Modern History and English Literature in Queen's College, Belfast. Crown 8vo. 7s. 6d.

Lectures on the Science of Language. By F. MAX MÜLLER, M.A. &c. Foreign Member of the French Institute. Sixth Edition. 2 vols. crown 8vo. price 16s.

Southey's Doctor, complete in One Volume, edited by the Rev. J. W. WARTER, B.D. Square crown 8vo. 12s. 6d.

Manual of English Literature, Historical and Critical with a Chapter on English Metres. By THOMAS ARNOLD, M.A. New Edition. Crown 8vo. 7s. 6d.

A Dictionary of Roman and Greek Antiquities. With about 2,000 Engravings on Wood, from Ancient Originals, illustrative of the Industrial Arts and Social Life of the Greeks and Romans. By ANTHONY RICH, B.A., sometime of Caius College, Cambridge. Third Edition, revised and improved. Crown 8vo. price 7s. 6d.

A Sanskrit-English Dictionary. The Sanskrit words printed both in the original Devanagari and in Roman letters; with References to the Best Editions of Sanskrit Authors, and with Etymologies and comparisons of Cognate Words chiefly in Greek, Latin, Gothic, and Anglo-Saxon. Compiled by T. BENFEY. 8vo. 52s. 6d.

A Latin-English Dictionary. By JOHN T. WHITE, D.D. Oxon. and J. E. RIDDLE, M.A. Oxon. Third Edition, revised. 2 vols. 4to. pp. 2,128, price 42s.

White's College Dictionary (Intermedia from the Parent Work versity Students. Medi price 18s.

White's Junior St plete Latin-English Dictionary. Revised 12mo. pp. 1,058, price 1:

Separately { ENGLISH
              LATIN-E

An English-Greek taining all the Greek Wo of good authority. By New Edition. 4to. 21s.

Mr. Yonge's New glish and Greek, abridg work (as above). Squar

A Greek-English 1 piled by H. G. LIDDE Christ Church, and R. of Rochester. Sixth E price 36s.

A Lexicon, Greek abridged for Schools f SCOTT's *Greek-English 1* Edition. Square 12mo.

The Mastery of L the Art of Speaking Idiomatically. By THO) late of the Civil Service (Edition. 8vo. 6s.

A Practical Dicti French and English L fessor LÉON CONTANS French Examiner for Appointments, &c. Nev revised. Post 8vo. 10s.

Contanseau's Pock French and English, Practical Dictionary, by Edition. 18mo. price 3s.

New Practical Dic German Language; Ge English-German. By BLACKLEY, M.A. and FRIEDLÄNDER. Post 8\

Historical and Crit tary on the Old Testa Translation. By M. M Vol. I. *Genesis*, 8vo. 18s General Reader, 12s. V or adapted for the Ge Vol III. *Leviticus*, Par for the General Reader, *ticus*, Part II. 15s. o: General Reader, 8s.

Miscellaneous Works and Popular Metaphysics.

An Introduction to Mental Philosophy, on the Inductive Method. By J. D. MORELL, M.A. LL.D. 8vo. 12s.

Elements of Psychology, containing the Analysis of the Intellectual Powers. By J. D. MORELL, LL.D. Post 8vo. 7s. 6d.

Recreations of a Country Parson. By A. K. H. B. Two Series, 3s. 6d. each.

Seaside Musings on Sundays and Weekdays. By A. K. H. B. Crown 8vo. price 3s. 6d.

Present-Day Thoughts. By A. K. H. B. Crown 8vo. 3s. 6d.

Changed Aspects of Unchanged Truths; Memorials of St. Andrews Sundays. By A. K. H. B. Crown 8vo. 3s. 6d.

Counsel and Comfort from a City Pulpit. By A. K. H. B. Crown 8vo. 3s. 6d.

Lessons of Middle Age, with some Account of various Cities and Men. By A. K. H. B. Crown 8vo. 3s. 6d.

Leisure Hours in Town; Essays Consolatory, Æsthetical, Moral, Social, and Domestic. By A. K. H. B. Crown 8vo. 3s. 6d.

Sunday Afternoons at the Parish Church of a Scottish University City. By A. K. H. B. Crown 8vo. 3s. 6d.

The Commonplace Philosopher in Town and Country. By A. K. H. B. 3s. 6d.

The Autumn Holidays of a Country Parson. By A. K. H. B. Crown 8vo. 3s. 6d.

Critical Essays of a Country Parson. By A. K. H. B. Crown 8vo. 3s. 6d.

The Graver Thoughts of a County Parson. By A. K. H. B. Two Series, 3s. 6d. each.

Miscellaneous and Posthumous Works of the late Henry Thomas Buckle. Edited, with a Biographical Notice, by HELEN TAYLOR. 3 vols. 8vo. price 2l. 12s. 6d.

In the Morningland, or the Law of the Origin and Transformation of Christianity; Travel and Discussion in the East with the late Henry Thomas Buckle. By JOHN S. STUART-GLENNIE, M.A. Post 8vo. [*In May.*

Short Studies on Great Subjects. By JAMES ANTHONY FROUDE, M.A. late Fellow of Exeter College, Oxford. 2 vols. crown 8vo. price 12s.

Miscellaneous Writings of John Conington, M.A. late Corpus Professor of Latin in the University of Oxford. Edited by J. A. SYMONDS, M.A. With a Memoir by H. J. S. SMITH, M.A. LL.D. F.R.S. 2 vols. 8vo. price 28s.

The Rev. Sydney Smith's Miscellaneous Works. Crown 8vo. price 6s.

The Wit and Wisdom of the Rev. SYDNEY SMITH; a Selection of the most memorable Passages in his Writings and Conversation. Crown 8vo. 3s. 6d.

The Eclipse of Faith; or, a Visit to a Religious Sceptic. By HENRY ROGERS. Twelfth Edition. Fcp. 8vo. 5s.

Defence of the Eclipse of Faith. By HENRY ROGERS. Third Edition. Fcp. 8vo. price 3s. 6d.

Lord Macaulay's Miscellaneous Writings:—
LIBRARY EDITION, 2 vols. 8vo. Portrait, 21s.
PEOPLE'S EDITION, 1 vol. crown 8vo. 4s. 6d.

Lord Macaulay's Miscellaneous Writings and Speeches. Student's Edition, in One Volume, crown 8vo. price 6s.

The Election of Representatives, Parliamentary and Municipal; a Treatise. By THOMAS HARE, Barrister-at-Law. Fourth Edition, adapting the proposed Law to the Ballot, with Appendices on the Preferential and the Cumulative Vote. Post 8vo. price 7s.

Chips from a German Workshop; being Essays on the Science of Religion, and on Mythology, Traditions, and Customs. By F. MAX MÜLLER, M.A. &c. Foreign Member of the French Institute. 3 vols. 8vo. £2.

A Budget of Paradoxes. By AUGUSTUS DE MORGAN, F.R.A.S. and C.P.S. of Trinity College, Cambridge. Reprinted, with the Author's Additions, from the *Athenæum*. 8vo. price 15s.

The Secret of Hegel: being the Hegelian System in Origin, Principle, Form, and Matter. By JAMES HUTCHISON STIRLING, LL.D. Edin. 2 vols. 8vo. 28s.

Lectures on the Philosophy of Law. Together with Whewell and Hegel, and Hegel and Mr. W. R. Smith; a Vindication in a Physico-Mathematical Regard. By J. H. STIRLING, LL.D. Edin. 8vo, price 6s.

As Regards Protoplasm. By J. H. STIRLING, LL.D. Edin. Second Edit., with Additions, in reference to Mr. Huxley's Second Issue and a new PREFACE in reply to Mr. Huxley in 'Yeast.' 8vo. price 2s.

Sir William Hamilton; being the Philosophy of Perception: an Analysis. By J. H. STIRLING, LL.D. Edin. 8vo. 5s.

The Philosophy of Necessity; or, Natural Law as applicable to Mental, Moral, and Social Science. By CHARLES BRAY. Second Edition. 8vo. 9s.

A Manual of Anthropology, or Sience of Man, based on Modern Research. By CHARLES BRAY. Crown 8vo. 6s.

On Force, its Mental and Moral Correlates. By CHARLES BRAY. 8vo. 5s.

Time and Space; a Metaphysical Essay. By SHADWORTH H. HODGSON. 8vo. price 16s.

The Theory of Practice; an Ethical Inquiry. By SHADWORTH H. HODGSON. 2 vols. 8vo. price 24s.

Ueberweg's System of Logic and History of Logical Doctrines. Translated, with Notes and Appendices, by T. M. LINDSAY, M.A. F.R.S.E. 8vo. price 16s.

The Senses and the Intellect. By ALEXANDER BAIN, LL.D. Prof. of Logic in the Univ. of Aberdeen. Third Edition. 8vo. 15s.

Mental and Moral Science: a Compendium of Psychology and Ethics By ALEXANDER BAIN, LL.D. Third Edition. Crown 8vo. 10s. 6d. Or separately: PART I. *Mental Science*, 6s. 6d. PART II. *Moral Science*, 4s. 6d.

A Treatise on Human Nature; being an Attempt to Introduce the Experimental Method of Reasoning into Moral Subjects. By DAVID HUME. Edited, with Notes, &c. by T. H. GREEN, Fellow, and T. H. GROSE, late Scholar, of Balliol College, Oxford. 2 vols. 8vo. [*In the press.*

Essays Moral, Political, and Literary. By DAVID HUME. By the same Editors. 2 vols. 8vo. [*In the press.*

Astronomy, Meteorology, Popular Geography, &c.

Outlines of Astronomy. By Sir J. F. W. HERSCHEL, Bart. M.A Eleventh Edition, with 9 Plates and numerous Diagrams. Square crown 8vo. 12s.

Essays on Astronomy. A Series of Papers on Planets and Meteors, the Sun and sun-surrounding Space, Stars and Star Cloudlets; and a Dissertation on the approaching Transit of Venus: preceded by a Sketch of the Life and Work of Sir J. Herschel. By R. A. PROCTOR, B.A. With 10 Plates and 24 Woodcuts. 8vo. price 12s.

Schellen's Spectrum Analysis, in its Application to Terrestrial Substances and the Physical Constitution of the Heavenly Bodies. Translated by JANE and C. LASSELL; edited, with Notes, by W. HUGGINS, LL.D. F.R.S. With 13 Plates (6 coloured) and 223 Woodcuts. 8vo. 28s.

The Sun; Ruler, Light, Fire, and Life of the Planetary System. By RICHARD A. PROCTOR, B.A. F.R.A.S. Second Edition; with 10 Plates (7 coloured) and 107 Woodcuts. Crown 8vo. price 14s.

Saturn and its System. By R. A. PROCTOR, B.A. 8vo. with 14 Plates, 14s.

Magnetism and Deviation of the Compass. For the use of Students in Navigation and Science Schools. By JOHN MERRIFIELD, LL.D. F.R.A.S. With Diagrams. 18mo. price 1s. 6d.

Air and Rain; the Beginnings of a Chemical Climatology. By ROBERT ANGUS SMITH, Ph.D. F.R.S. F.C.S. Government Inspector of Alkali Works, with Illustrations. 8vo. price 24s.

The Star Depths; or, other Suns than Ours; a Treatise on Stars, Star-Systems, and Star-Cloudlets. By R. A. PROCTOR, B.A. Crown 8vo. with numerous Illustrations. [*Nearly ready.*

The Orbs Around Us; a Series of Familiar Essays on the Moon and Planets Meteors and Comets, the Sun and Coloured Pairs of Suns. By R. A. PROCTOR, B.A. Crown 8vo. price 7s. 6d.

Other Worlds than Ours; the Plurality of Worlds Studied under the Light of Recent Scientific Researches. By R. A. PROCTOR, B.A. Third Edition revised and corrected; with 14 Illustrations. Crown 8vo. 10s. 6d.

Celestial Objects for Common Telescopes. By T. W. WEBB, M.A. F.R.A.S. New Edition, revised, with Map of the Moon and Woodcuts. Crown 8vo. price 7s. 6d.

A New Star Atlas, for the Library, the School, and the Observatory, in Twelve Circular Maps (with Two Index Plates) Intended as a Companion to 'Webb's Celestial Objects for Common Telescopes.' With a Letterpress Introduction on the Study of the Stars, illustrated by 9 Diagrams. By RICHARD A. PROCTOR, B.A. Hon. Sec. R.A.S. Crown 8vo. 5s.

Maunder's Treasury of Geography, Physical, Historical, Descriptive, and Political. Edited by W. HUGHES, F.R.G.S. With 7 Maps and 16 Plates. Fcp. 8vo. 6s.

A General Dictionary of Geography, Descriptive, Physical, Statistical, and Historical; forming a complete Gazetteer of the World. By A. KEITH JOHNSTON, F.R.S.E. New Edition, thoroughly revised. [*In the press.*

The Public Schools Atlas of Modern Geography. In Thirty-one Maps, exhibiting clearly the more important Physical Features of the Countries delineated, and Noting all the Chief Places of Historical, Commercial, and Social Interest. Edited, with an Introduction, by the Rev. G. BUTLER, M.A. Imperial quarto, price 3s. 6d. sewed; 5s. cloth.

Nautical Surveying, an Introduction to the Practical and Theoretical Study of. By JOHN KNOX LAUGHTON, M.A. F.R.A.S. Small 8vo. price 6s.

Natural History and *Popular Science.*

Popular Lectures on Scientific Subjects. By H. HELMHOLTZ, Professor of Physiology, formerly in the University of Heidelberg, and now in the University of Berlin, Foreign Member of the Royal Society of London. Translated by E. ATKINSON Ph.D. F.C.S Professor of Experimental Science, Staff College. With many Illustrative Wood Engravings. 8vo. price 12s. 6d.

Introduction to Experimental Physics, Theoretical and Practical; including Directions for Constructing Physical Apparatus and for Making Experiments. By A. F. WEINHOLD, Professor in the Royal Technical School at Chemnitz. Translated and edited (with the Author's sanction) by B. LOEWY, F.R.A.S. With a Preface by G. C. FOSTER, F.R.S. Professor of Physics in University College, London. With numerous Wood Engravings. 8vo. price 18s.

Natural Philosophy for General Readers and Young Persons; a Course of Physics divested of Mathematical Formulæ and expressed in the language of daily life. Translated from Ganot's *Cours de Physique*, by E. ATKINSON, Ph.D. F.C.S. Crown 8vo. with 404 Woodcuts, price 7s. 6d.

Mrs. Marcet's Conversations on Natural Philosophy. Revised by the Author's Son, and augmented by Conversations on Spectrum Analysis and Solar Chemistry. With 36 Plates. Crown 8vo. price 7s. 6d.

Ganot's Elementary Treatise on Physics, Experimental and Applied, for the use of Colleges and Schools. Translated and Edited with the Author's sanction by E. ATKINSON, Ph.D. F.C.S. New Edition, revised and enlarged; with a Coloured Plate and 726 Woodcuts. Post 8vo. 15s.

Text-Books of Science, Mechanical and, Physical. Edited by T. M. GOODEVE, M.A. and C. W. MERRIFIELD, F.R.S. Small 8vo. price 3s. 6d. each:—
1. GOODEVE's Mechanism.
2. BLOXAM's Metals.
3. MILLER's Inorganic Chemistry.
4. GRIFFIN's Algebra and Trigonometry. GRIFFIN's Notes and Solutions.
5. WATSON's Plane and Solid Geometry.
6. MAXWELL's Theory of Heat.
7. MERRIFIELD's Technical Arithmetic and Mensuration.
 KEY, by the Rev. JOHN HUNTER, M.A.
8. ANDERSON's Strength of Materials.
9. JENKIN's Electricity and Magnetism.

Dove's Law of Storms, considered in connexion with the ordinary Movements of the Atmosphere. Translated by R. H. SCOTT, M.A. T.C.D. 8vo. 10s. 6d.

The Correlation of Physical Forces. By Sir W. R. GROVE, Q.C. V.P.R.S Fifth Edition, revised, and Augmented by a Discourse on Continuity. 8vo. 10s. 6d.

Fragments of Science. By JOHN TYNDALL, LL.D. F.R.S. Third Edition 8vo. price 14s.

B

Heat a Mode of Motion. By JOHN TYNDALL, LL.D. F.R.S. Fourth Edition. Crown 8vo. with Woodcuts, price 10s. 6d.

Sound; a Course of Eight Lectures delivered at the Royal Institution of Great Britain. By JOHN TYNDALL, LL.D. F.R.S. New Edition, with Portrait and Woodcuts. Crown 8vo. 9s.

Researches on Diamagnetism and Magne-Crystallic Action; including the Question of Diamagnetic Polarity. By JOHN TYNDALL, LL.D. F.R.S. With 6 Plates and many Woodcuts. 8vo. 14s.

Principles of Animal Mechanics. By the Rev. SAMUEL HAUGHTON, F.R.S. M.D. Dublin, D.C.L. Oxon. Fellow of Trinity College, Dublin. 8vo. price 21s.

Lectures on Light, Delivered in America in 1872 and 1873. By JOHN TYNDALL, LL.D., F.R S. Professor of Natural Philosophy in the Royal Insitution of Great Britain. [*In the press.*

Notes of a Course of Nine Lectures on Light, delivered at the Royal Institution, A.D. 1869. By J. TYNDALL, LL.D. F.R.S. Crown 8vo. 1s. sewed, or 1s. 6d. cloth.

Notes of a Course of Seven Lectures on Electrical Phenomena and Theories, delivered at the Royal Institution, A.D. 1870. By JOHN TYNDALL, LL.D. F.R.S. Crown 8vo. 1s. sewed, or 1s. 6d. cloth.

Light Science for Leisure Hours; a Series of Familiar Essays on Scientific Subjects, Natural Phenomena, &c. By R. A. PROCTOR, B.A. Second Edition, revised. Crown 8vo. price 7s. 6d.

Light: its Influence on Life and Health. By FORBES WINSLOW, M.D. D.C.L. Oxon. (Hon.) Fcp. 8vo. 6s.

Professor Owen's Lectures on the Comparative Anatomy and Physiology of the Invertebrate Animals. Second Edition, with 235 Woodcuts. 8vo. 21s.

The Comparative Anatomy and Physiology of the Vertebrate Animals. By RICHARD OWEN, F.R.S. D.C.L. With 1,472 Woodcuts. 3 vols. 8vo. £3 13s. 6d.

Kirby and Spence's Introduction to Entomology, or Elements of the Natural History of Insects. Crown 8vo. 5s.

Strange Dwellings; a Description of the Habitations of Animals, abridged from 'Homes without Hands.' By J. G. WOOD, M.A. F.L.S. With a New Frontispiece and about 60 other Woodcut Illustrations. Crown 8vo. price 7s. 6d.

Homes without Hands; a Description of the Habitations of Animals, classed according to their Principle of Construction. By Rev. J. G. WOOD, M.A. F.L.S. With about 140 Vignettes on Wood. 8vo. 21s.

The Harmonies of Nature and Unity of Creation. By Dr. G. HARTWIG. 8vo. with numerous Illustrations, 18s.

The Aerial World. By Dr. GEORGE HARTWIG, Author of 'The Sea and its Living Wonders,' 'The Polar World,' &c. 8vo. with numerous Illustrations. [*In the press.*

The Sea and its Living Wonders. By the same Author. Third Edition, enlarged. 8vo. with many Illustrations, 21s.

The Tropical World; a Popular Scientific Account of the Natural History of the Equatorial Regions. By the same Author. New Edition, with about 200 Illustrations. 8vo. price 10s. 6d.

The Subterranean World. By the same Author. With 3 Maps and about 80 Woodcut Illustrations, including 8 full size of page. 8vo. price 21s.

The Polar World: a Popular Description of Man and Nature in the Arctic and Antarctic Regions of the Globe. By the same Author. With 8 Chromoxylographs, 3 Maps, and 85 Woodcuts. 8vo. 21s.

A Familiar History of Birds. By E. STANLEY, D.D. late Lord Bishop of Norwich. Fcp. with Woodcuts, 3s. 6d.

Insects at Home; a Popular Account of British Insects, their Structure, Habits, and Transformations. By the Rev. J. G. WOOD, M.A. F.L.S. With upwards of 700 Illustrations engraved on Wood. 8vo. price 21s.

Insects Abroad; being a Popular Account of Foreign Insects, their Structure, Habits, and Transformations. By J. G. WOOD, M.A. F.L.S. Author of 'Homes without Hands' &c. In One Volume, printed and illustrated uniformly with 'Insects at Home,' to which it will form a Sequel and Companion. [*In the press.*

The Primitive Inhabitants of Scandinavia. Containing a Description of the Implements, Dwellings, Tombs, and Mode of Living of the Savages in the North of Europe during the Stone Age. By SVEN NILSSON. 8vo. Plates and Woodcuts, 18s.

The Origin of Civilisation, and the Primitive Condition of Man; Mental and Social Condition of Savages. By Sir JOHN LUBBOCK, Bart. M.P. F.R.S. Second Edition, with 25 Woodcuts. 8vo. 16s.

An Exposition of Fallacies in the Hypothesis of Mr. Darwin. By C. R. BREE, M.D. F.Z.S. With 36 Woodcuts. Crown 8vo. price 14s.

The Ancient Stone Implements, Weapons, and Ornaments, of Great Britain. By JOHN EVANS, F.R.S. F.S.A. 8vo. with 2 Plates and 476 Woodcuts, price 28s.

Mankind, their Origin and Destiny. By an M.A. of Balliol College, Oxford. Containing a New Translation of the First Three Chapters of Genesis; a Critical Examination of the First Two Gospels; an Explanation of the Apocalypse; and the Origin and Secret Meaning of the Mythological and Mystical Teaching of the Ancients. With 31 Illustrations. 8vo. price 31s. 6d.

Bible Animals; a Description of every Living Creature mentioned in the Scriptures, from the Ape to the Coral. By the Rev. J. G. WOOD, M.A. F.L.S. With about 100 Vignettes on Wood. 8vo. 21s.

Maunder's Treasury of Natural History, or Popular Dictionary of Zoology. Revised and corrected Edition. Fcp. 8vo. with 900 Woodcuts, price 6s.

The Elements of Botany for Families and Schools. Tenth Edition, revised by THOMAS MOORE, F.L.S. Fcp. with 154 Woodcuts, 2s. 6d.

The Treasury of Botany, or Popular Dictionary of the Vegetable Kingdom; with which is incorporated a Glossary of Botanical Terms. Edited by J. LINDLEY, F.R.S. and T. MOORE, F.L.S. Pp. 1,274, with 274 Woodcuts and 20 Steel Plates. TWO PARTS, fcp. 8vo. 12s.

The Rose Amateur's Guide. By THOMAS RIVERS. The Tenth Edition, revised and improved. Fcp. 8vo. price 4s.

A Dictionary of Science, Literature, and Art. Fourth Edition, re-edited by the late W. T. BRANDE (the Author) and GEORGE W. COX, M.A. 3 vols. medium 8vo. price 63s. cloth.

Maunder's Scientific and Literary Treasury; a Popular Encyclopædia of Science, Literature, and Art. New Edition, in part rewritten, with above 1,000 new articles, by J. Y. JOHNSON. Fcp. 6s.

Loudon's Encyclopædia of Plants; comprising the Specific Character, Description, Culture, History, &c. of all the Plants found in Great Britain. With upwards of 12,000 Woodcuts. 8vo. 42s.

Handbook of Hardy Trees, Shrubs, and Herbaceous Plants; containing Descriptions, Native Countries, &c. of a selection of the Best Species in Cultivation; together with Cultural Details, Comparative Hardiness, suitability for particular positions, &c. Based on the French Work of Messrs. DECAISNE and NAUDIN, intitled 'Manuel de l'Amateur des Jardins,' and including 720 Woodcut Illustrations by Riocreux and Leblanc. By W. B. HEMSLEY, formerly Assistant at the Herbarium of the Royal Gardens, Kew. Medium 8vo. 21s.

A General System of Descriptive and Analytical Botany: I. Organography, Anatomy, and Physiology of Plants; II. Iconography, or the Description and History of Natural Families. Translated from the French of E. LE MAOUT, M.D. and J. DECAISNE, Member of the Institute, by Mrs. HOOKER. Edited and arranged according to the Botanical System adopted in the Universities and Schools of Great Britain, by J. D. HOOKER, M.D. &c. Director of the Royal Botanic Gardens, Kew. With 5,500 Woodcuts from Designs by L. Stenheil and A. Riocreux. Medium 8vo. price 52s. 6d.

Chemistry, Medicine, Surgery, and the Allied Sciences.

A Dictionary of Chemistry and the Allied Branches of other Sciences. By HENRY WATTS, F.C.S. assisted by eminent Scientific and Practical Chemists. 5 vols. medium 8vo. price £7 3s.

Supplement, Completing the Record of Discovery to the end of 1869. 8vo. 31s. 6d.

Contributions to Molecular Physics in the domain of Radiant Heat; a Series of Memoirs published in the Philosophical Transactions, &c. By JOHN TYNDALL, LL.D. F.R.S. With 2 Plates and 31 Woodcuts. 8vo. price 16s.

Elements of Chemistry, Theoretical and Practical. By WILLIAM A MILLER, M.D. LL.D. Professor of Chemistry, King's College, London. New Edition. 3 vols. 8vo. £3.

PART I. CHEMICAL PHYSICS, 15s.
PART II. INORGANIC CHEMISTRY, 21s.
PART III. ORGANIC CHEMISTRY, 24s.

A Course of Practical Chemistry, for the use of Medical Students. By W. ODLING, M.B. F.R.S. New Edition, will 70 new Woodcuts. Crown 8vo. 7s. 6d.

A Manual of Chemical Physiology, including its Points of Contact with Pathology. By J. L. W. THUDICHUM, M.D. 8vo. with Woodcuts, price 7s. 6d.

Select Methods in Chemical Analysis, chiefly Inorganic. By WILLIAM CROOKES, F.R.S. With 22 Woodcuts. Crown 8vo. price 12s. 6d.

Chemical Notes for the Lecture Room. By THOMAS WOOD, F.C.S. 2 vols. crown 8vo. I. on Heat, &c. price 5s. II. on the Metals, price 5s.

The Handbook for Midwives. By HENRY FLY SMITH, B.A. M.B. Oxon. M.R.C.S. Eng. late Assistant-Surgeon at the Hospital for Women, Soho Square. With 41 Woodcuts. Crown 8vo. price 5s.

The Diagnosis, Pathology, and Treatment of Diseases of Women; including the Diagnosis of Pregnancy. By GRAILY HEWITT, M.D. &c. Third Edition, revised and for the most part re-written; with 132 Woodcuts. 8vo. 24s.

Lectures on the Diseases of Infancy and Childhood. By CHARLES WEST, M.D. &c. Fifth Edition. 8vo. 16s.

On Some Disorders of the Nervous System in Childhood. Being the Lumleian Lectures delivered before the Royal College of Physicians in March 1871 By CHARLES WEST, M.D. Crown 8vo. 5s

On Chronic Bronchitis, especially as connected with Gout, Emphysema, and Diseases of the Heart. By E. HEADLAM GREENHOW, M.D. F.R.S. Physician to and Lecturer on the Principles and Practice of Medicine at the Middlesex Hospital. 8vo. price 7s. 6d.

On the Surgical Treatment of Children's Diseases. By T. HOLMES, M.A. &c. late Surgeon to the Hospital for Sick Children. Second Edition, with 9 Plates and 112 Woodcuts. 8vo. 21s.

Lectures on the Principles and Practice of Physic. By Sir THOMAS WATSON, Bart. M.D. Physician-in-Ordinary to the Queen. Fifth Edition, thoroughly revised. 2 vols. 8vo. price 36s.

Lectures on Surgical Pathology. By Sir JAMES PAGET, Bart. F.R.S. Third Edition, revised and re-edited by the Author and Professor W. TURNER, M.B. 8vo. with 131 Woodcuts. 21s.

Cooper's Dictionary of Practical Surgery and Encyclopædia of Surgical Science. New Edition, brought down to the present time. By S. A. LANE, Surgeon to St. Mary's Hospital, &c. assisted by various Eminent Surgeons. 2 vols. 8vo. price 25s. each.

Pulmonary Consumption; its Nature, Varieties, and Treatment: with an Analysis of One Thousand Cases to exemplify its Duration. By C. J. B. WILLIAMS, M.D. F.R.S. and C. T. WILLIAMS, M.A. M.D. Oxon. Post 8vo. price 10s. 6d.

The Climate of the South of France as suited to Invalids; with Notices of Mediterranean and other Winter Stations. By C. T. WILLIAMS, M.D. Physician to the Hospital for Consumption at Brompton. Second Edition, with an Appendix on Alpine Summer Quarters and the Mountain Cure, and a Map. Crown 8vo. price 6s.

Anatomy, Descriptive and Surgical. By HENRY GRAY, F.R.S. With about 410 Woodcuts from Dissections. Sixth Edition, by T. HOLMES, M.A. Cantab. With a New Introduction by the Editor. Royal 8vo. 28s.

The House I Live in; or, Popular Illustrations of the Structure and Functions of the Human Body. Edited by T. G. GIRTIN New Edition, with 25 Woodcuts. 16mo. price 2s. 6d.

Quain's Elements of Anatomy. Seventh Edition [1867]. Edited by W. SHARPEY, M.D. F.R.S. Professor of Anatomy and Physiology in University College, London; ALLEN THOMAS, M.D. F.R.S. Professor of Anatomy in the University of Glasgow: and J. CLELAND, M.D. Professor of Anatomy in Queen's College, Galway. With upwards of 800 Engravings on Wood. 2 vols. 8vo. price 31s. 6d.

The Science and Art of Surgery; being a Treatise on Surgical Injuries, Diseases, and Operations. By JOHN ERIC ERICHSEN, Senior Surgeon to University College Hospital, and Holme Professor of Clinical Surgery in University College, London. A New Edition, being the Sixth, revised and enlarged; with 712 Woodcuts. 2 vols. 8vo. price 32s.

A System of Surgery, Theoretical and Practical, in Treatises by Various Authors. Edited by T. HOLMES, M.A. &c. Surgeon and Lecturer on Surgery at St. George's Hospital, and Surgeon-in-Chief to the Metropolitan Police. Second Edition, thoroughly revised, with numerous Illustrations. 5 vols. 8vo. £5 5s.

A Treatise on the Continued Fevers of Great Britain. By CHARLES MURCHISON, M.D. New Edition, revised. [*Nearly ready.*

Clinical Lectures on Diseases of the Liver, Jaundice, and Abdominal Dropsy. By CHARLES MURCHISON, M.D. Physician to the Middlesex Hospital. Post 8vo. with 25 Woodcuts. 10s. 6d.

Copland's Dictionary of Practical Medicine, abridged from the larger work, and throughout brought down to the present state of Medical Science. 8vo. 36s.

Outlines of Physiology, Human and Comparative. By JOHN MARSHALL, F.R.C.S. Surgeon to the University College Hospital. 2 vols. crown 8vo. with 122 Woodcuts, 32s.

Dr. Pereira's Elements of Materia Medica and Therapeutics, abridged and adapted for the use of Medical and Pharmaceutical Practitioners and Students. Edited by Professor BENTLEY, F.L.S. &c. and by Dr. REDWOOD, F.C.S. &c. With 125 Woodcut Illustrations. 8vo. price 25s.

The Essentials of Materia Medica and Therapeutics. By ALFRED BARING GARROD, M.D. F.R.S. &c. Physician to King's College Hospital. Third Edition Sixth Impression, brought up to 1870. Crown 8vo. price 12s. 6d.

Todd and Bowman's Physiological Anatomy and Physiology of Man. With numerous Illustrations. VOL. II. 8vo. price 25s.

VOL. I. New Edition by Dr. LIONEL S. BEALE, F.R.S. in course of publication, with numerous Illustrations. PARTS I. and II. price 7s. 6d. each.

The Fine Arts, and *Illustrated Editions*.

Grotesque Animals, invented, described, and portrayed by E. W. COOKE, R.A. F.R.S. F.GS. F.Z.S. in 24 Plates, with Elucidatory Comments. Royal 4to. 21s.

In Fairyland; Pictures from the Elf-World. By RICHARD DOYLE. With a Poem by W. ALLINGHAM. With 16 coloured Plates, containing 36 Designs. Folio, 31s. 6d.

Albert Durer, his Life and Works; including Autobiographical Papers and Complete Catalogues. By WILLIAM B. SCOTT. With Six Etchings by the Author and other Illustrations. 8vo. 16s.

Half-Hour Lectures on the History and Practice of the Fine and Ornamental Arts. By. W. B. SCOTT. Second Edition. Crown 8vo. with 50 Woodcut Illustrations, 8s. 6d.

The Chorale Book for England: the Hymns Translated by Miss C. WINKWORTH; the Tunes arranged by Prof. W. S. BENNETT and OTTO GOLDSCHMIDT. Fcp. 4to. 12s. 6d.

The New Testament, illustrated with Wood Engravings after the Early Masters, chiefly of the Italian School. Crown 4to. 63s. cloth, gilt top; or £5 5s. morocco.

The Life of Man Symbolised by the Months of the Year in their Seasons and Phases. Text selected by RICHARD PIGOT. 25 Illustrations on Wood from Original Designs by JOHN LEIGHTON, F.S.A. Quarto, 42s.

Cats and Farlie's Moral Emblems; with Aphorisms, Adages, and Proverbs of all Nations: comprising 121 Illustrations on Wood by J. LEIGHTON, F.S.A. with an appropriate Text by R. PIGOT. Imperial 8vo. 31s. 6d.

Sacred and Legendary Art. By Mrs. JAMESON. 6 vols. square crown 8vo. price £5 15s. 6d. as follows:—

Legends of the Saints and Martyrs. New Edition, with 19 Etchings and 187 Woodcuts. 2 vols. price 31s. 6d.

Legends of the Monastic Orders. New Edition, with 11 Etchings and 88 Woodcuts. 1 vol. price 21s.

Legends of the Madonna. New Edition, with 27 Etchings and 165 Woodcuts. 1 vol. price 21s.

The History of Our Lord, with that of His Types and Precursors. Completed by Lady EASTLAKE. Revised Edition, with 13 Etchings and 281 Woodcuts. 2 vols. price 42s.

Lyra Germanica, the Christian Year. Translated by CATHERINE WINKWORTH, with 125 Illustrations on Wood drawn by J. LEIGHTON, F.S.A. Quarto, 21s.

Lyra Germanica, the Christian Life. Translated by CATHERINE WINKWORTH; with about 200 Woodcut Illustrations by J. LEIGHTON, F.S.A. and other Artists. Quarto, 21s.

The Useful Arts, Manufactures, &c.

Gwilt's Encyclopædia of Architecture, with above 1,600 Woodcuts. Fifth Edition, with Alterations and considerable Additions, by WYATT PAPWORTH. 8vo. price 52s. 6d.

A Manual of Architecture: being a Concise History and Explanation of the principal Styles of European Architecture, Ancient, Mediæval, and Renaissance; with their Chief Variations and a Glossary of Technical Terms. By THOMAS MITCHELL. With 150 Woodcuts. Crown 8vo. 10s. 6d.

History of the Gothic Revival; an Attempt to shew how far the taste for Mediæval Architecture was retained in England during the last two centuries, and has been re-developed in the present. By C. L. EASTLAKE, Architect. With 48 Illustrations (36 full size of page). Imperial 8vo. price 31s. 6d.

Hints on Household Taste in Furniture, Upholstery, and other Details. By CHARLES L. EASTLAKE, Architect. New Edition, with about 90 Illustrations. Square crown 8vo. 14s.

Geometric Turning: comprising a Description of the New Geometric Chuck constructed by Mr. Plant of Birmingham, with Directions for its use, and a Series of Patterns cut by it; with Explanations of the mode of producing them, and an Account of a New Process of Deep Cutting and of Graving on Copper. By H. S. SAVORY. With 571 Woodcut Illustrations. Square crown 8vo. price 21s.

Lathes and Turning, Simple, Mechanical, and Ornamental. By W. HENRY NORTHCOTT. With about 240 Illustrations on Steel and Wood. 8vo, 18s.

Perspective; or, the Art of Drawing what one Sees. Explained and adapted to the use of those Sketching from Nature. By Lieut. W. H. COLLINS, R.E. F.R.A.S. With 37 Woodcuts. Crown 8vo. price 5s.

Principles of Mechanism, designed for the use of Students in the Universities, and for Engineering Students generally. By R. WILLIS, M.A. F.R.S. &c. Jacksonian Professor in the Univ. of Cambridge. Second Edition; with 374 Woodcuts. 8vo. 18s.

Handbook of Practical Telegraphy. By R. S. CULLEY, Memb. Inst. C.E. Engineer-in-Chief of Telegraphs to the Post-Office. Fifth Edition, revised and enlarged; with 118 Woodcuts and 9 Plates. 8vo. price 14s.

Ure's Dictionary of Arts, Manufactures, and Mines. Sixth Edition, re written and greatly enlarged by ROBER HUNT, F.R.S. assisted by numerous Con tributors. With 2,000 Woodcuts. 3 vols medium 8vo. £4 14s. 6d.

Encyclopædia of Civil Engineer ing, Historical, Theoretical, and Practical By E. CRESY, C.E. With above 3,00 Woodcuts. 8vo. 42s.

Catechism of the Steam Engine in its various Applications to Mines, Mills Steam Navigation, Railways, and Agricul ture. By JOHN BOURNE, C.E. New Edi tion, with 89 Woodcuts. Fcp. 8vo. 6s.

Handbook of the Steam Engine By JOHN BOURNE, C.E. forming a KEY t the Author's Catechism of the Steam Engine With 67 Woodcuts. Fcp. 8vo. price 9s.

Recent Improvements in the Steam Engine. By JOHN BOURNE, C.E New Edition, including many New Ex amples, with 124 Woodcuts. Fcp. 8vo. 6s.

A Treatise on the Steam Engine in its various Applications to Mines, Mills Steam Navigation, Railways, and Agri culture. By J. BOURNE, C.E. New Edition with Portrait, 37 Plates, and 546 Woodcut 4to. 42s.

Treatise on Mills and Millwork By Sir W. FAIRBAIRN, Bart. F.R.S. Nev Edition, with 18 Plates and 322 Woodcuts 2 vols. 8vo. 32s.

Useful Information for Engi neers. By the same Author. FIRST, SECONE and THIRD SERIES, with many Plates an Woodcuts. 3 vols. crown 8vo. 10s. 6d. each

The Application of Cast and Wrought Iron to Building Purposes. B the same Author. Fourth Edition, with Plates and 118 Woodcuts. 8vo. 16s.

The Strains in Trusses Computed by means of Diagrams; with 20 Example drawn to Scale. By F. A. RANKEN, M.A C.E. Lecturer at the Hartley Institution Southampton. With 35 Diagrams. Squar crown 8vo. price 6s. 6d.

Mitchell's Manual of Practical Assaying. New Edition, being the Fourth thoroughly revised, with the recent Dis coveries incorporated. By W. CROOKES F.R.S. With numerous Woodcuts. 8vo.
[*Nearly ready.*

Bayldon's Art of Valuing Rents and Tillages, and Claims of Tenants upon Quitting Farms, both at Michaelmas and Lady-Day. Eighth Edition, revised by J. C. MORTON. 8vo. 10s. 6d.

On the Manufacture of Beet-Root Sugar in England and Ireland. By WILLIAM CROOKES, F.R.S. With 11 Woodcuts. 8vo. 8s. 6d.

Loudon's Encyclopædia of Gardening: comprising the Theory and Practice of Horticulture, Floriculture, Arboriculture, and Landscape Gardening. With 1,000 Woodcuts. 8vo. 21s.

Practical Treatise on Metallurgy, adapted from the last German Edition of Professor KERL's *Metallurgy* by W. CROOKES, F.R.S. &c. and E. RÖHRIG, Ph.D. M.E. 3 vols. 8vo. with 625 Woodcuts, price 4l. 19s.

Loudon's Encyclopædia of Agriculture: comprising the Laying-out, Improvement, and Management of Landed Property, and the Cultivation and Economy of the Productions of Agriculture. With 1,100 Woodcuts. 8vo. 21s.

Religious and Moral Works.

The Speaker's Bible Commentary, by Bishops and other Clergy of the Anglican Church, critically examined by the Right Rev. J. W. COLENSO, D.D. Bishop of Natal. 8vo. PART I, *Genesis*, 3s. 6d. PART II. *Exodus*, 4s. 6d. PART III. *Leviticus*, 2s. 6d. PART IV. *Numbers*, 3s. 6d. PART V. *Deuteronomy*, 5s.

The Outlines of the Christian Ministry Delineated, and brought to the Test of Reason, Holy Scripture, History, and Experience. By CHRISTOPHER WORDSWORTH, D.C.L. &c. Bishop of St. Andrew's. Crown 8vo. price 7s. 6d.

Christian Counsels, selected from the Devotional Works of Fénélon, Archbishop of Cambrai. Translated by A. M. JAMES. Crown 8vo. price 5s.

Eight Essays on Ecclesiastical Reform. By various Writers; with Preface and Analysis of the Essays. Edited by the Rev. ORBY SHIPLEY, M.A. Crown 8vo. 10s. 6d.

Authority and Conscience; a Free Debate on the Tendency of Dogmatic Theology and on the Characteristics of Faith. Edited by CONWAY MOREL. Post 8vo. 7s. 6d.

Reasons of Faith; or, the Order of the Christian Argument Developed and Explained. By the Rev. G. S. DREW, M.A. Second Edition, revised and enlarged. Fcp. 8vo. 6s.

Christ the Consoler; a Book of Comfort for the Sick. With a Preface by the Right Rev. the Lord Bishop of Carlisle. Small 8vo. 6s.

The True Doctrine of the Eucharist. By THOMAS S. L. VOGAN, D.D. Canon and Prebendary of Chichester and Rural Dean. vo. 18s.

The Student's Compendium of the Book of Common Prayer; being Notes Historical and Explanatory of the Liturgy of the Church of England. By the Rev. H. ALLDEN NASH. Fcp. 8vo. price 2s. 6d.

Synonyms of the Old Testament, their Bearing on Christian Faith and Practice. By the Rev. ROBERT B. GIRDLESTONE, M.A. 8vo. price 15s.

Fundamentals; or, Bases of Belief concerning Man and God: a Handbook of Mental, Moral, and Religious Philosophy. By the Rev. T. GRIFFITH, M.A. 8vo. price 10s. 6d.

An Introduction to the Theology of the Church of England, in an Exposition of the Thirty-nine Articles. By the Rev. T. P. BOULTBEE, LL.D. Fcp. 8vo. price 6s.

Christian Sacerdotalism, viewed from a Layman's standpoint or tried by Holy Scripture and the Early Fathers; with a short Sketch of the State of the Church from the end of the Third to the Reformation in the beginning of the Sixteenth Century. By JOHN JARDINE, M.A. LL.D. 8vo. 8s. 6d.

Prayers for the Family and for Private Use, selected from the Collection of the late Baron BUNSEN, and Translated by CATHERINE WINKWORTH. Fcp. 8vo. price 3s. 6d.

Churches and their Creeds. By the Rev. Sir PHILIP PERRING, Bart. late Scholar of Trin. Coll. Cambridge, and University Medallist. Crown 8vo. 10s.

The Problem of the World and the Church Reconsidered, in Three Letters to a Friend. By a SEPTUAGENARIAN. Second Edition, revised and edited by JAMES BOOTH, C.B. Crown 8vo. price 5s.

An Exposition of the 39 Articles, Historical and Doctrinal. By E. HAROLD BROWNE, D.D. Lord Bishop of Ely. Ninth Edition. 8vo. 16s.

The Voyage and Shipwreck of St. Paul; with Dissertations on the Ships and Navigation of the Ancients. By JAMES SMITH, F.R.S. Crown 8vo. Charts, 10s. 6d.

The Life and Epistles of St. Paul. By the Rev. W. J. CONYBEARE, M.A. and the Very Rev. J. S. HOWSON, D.D. Dean of Chester. Three Editions:—

LIBRARY EDITION, with all the Original Illustrations, Maps, Landscapes on Steel, Woodcuts, &c. 2 vols. 4to. 48s.

INTERMEDIATE EDITION, with a Selection of Maps, Plates, and Woodcuts. 2 vols. square crown 8vo. 21s.

STUDENT'S EDITION, revised and condensed, with 46 Illustrations and Maps. 1 vol. crown 8vo. 9s.

Evidence of the Truth of the Christian Religion derived from the Literal Fulfilment of Prophecy. By ALEXANDER KEITH, D.D. 40th Edition, with numerous Plates, in square 8vo. 12s. 6d.; also the 39th Edition, in post 8vo. with 5 Plates, 6s.

The History and Destiny of the World and of the Church, according to Scripture. By the same Author. Square 8vo. with 40 Illustrations, 10s.

The History and Literature of the Israelites, according to the Old Testament and the Apocrypha. By C. DE ROTHSCHILD and A. DE ROTHSCHILD. Second Edition. 2 vols. crown 8vo. 12s. 6d. Abridged Edition, in 1 vol. fcp. 8vo. 3s. 6d.

Ewald's History of Israel to the Death of Moses. Translated from the German. Edited, with a Preface and an Appendix, by RUSSELL MARTINEAU, M.A. Second Edition. 2 vols. 8vo. 24s. Vols. III. and IV. edited by J. E. CARPENTER, M.A. price 21s.

England and Christendom. By ARCHBISHOP MANNING, D.D. Post 8vo. price 10s 6d.

Ignatius Loyola and the Early Jesuits. By STEWART ROSE New Edition, revised. 8vo. with Portrait, 16s.

An Introduction to the Study of the New Testament, Critical, Exegetical, and Theological. By the Rev. S. DAVIDSON, D.D. LL.D. 2 vols. 8vo. 30s.

Commentary on t] the Romans. By the Re B.A. Crown 8vo. price

The Epistle to t: With Analytical Introd By the Rev. W. A. O'Co 8vo. price 4s. 6d.

A Critical and Gran mentary on St. Paul's ELLICOTT, D.D. Lord B] and Bristol. 8vo.

Galatians, Fourth Editio:
Ephesians, Fourth Editi
Pastoral Epistles, Four
Philippians, Colossian: Third Edition, 10s. 6d.
Thessalonians, Third Ed

Historical Lectures Our Lord Jesus Christ : Lectures for 1859. By C Fifth Edition. 8vo. 12s

The Greek Testame Grammatical and Exege W. WEBSTER, M.A. an WILKINSON, M.A. 2 vc

The Treasury of ledge; being a Diction Persons, Places, Events, of which mention is m: ture. By Rev. J. A Maps, 15 Plates; and n Fcp. 8vo. price 6s.

Every-day Scriptur explained and illustrated COTT, M.A. I. *Matthew* a and *John*. 2 vols. 8vo.]

The Pentateuch Joshua Critically Exami Rev. J. W. COLENSO, L Natal. Crown 8vo. pric
PART V. Genesis Analy: and the Ages of its W 8vo. 18s.
PART VI. The Later L Pentateuch. 8vo. 24s.

The Formation of By T. W. ALLIES. PAI price 12s. each.

Four Discourses of chiefly on the parable of Lazarus. Translated by Crown 8vo. 3s. 6d.

Thoughts for the Ag M. SEWELL, Author of New Edition. Fcp. 8vo.

Passing Thoughts By Miss SEWELL. Fcp.

Self-examination before Confirmation. By Miss SEWELL. 32mo. 1s. 6d.

Thoughts for the Holy Week, for Young Persons. By Miss SEWELL. New Edition. Fcp. 8vo. 2s.

Readings for a Month Preparatory to Confirmation, from Writers of the Early and English Church. By Miss SEWELL. Fcp. 8vo. 4s.

Readings for Every Day in Lent, compiled from the Writings of Bishop JEREMY TAYLOR. By Miss SEWELL. Fcp. 5s.

Preparation for the Holy Communion; the Devotions chiefly from the works of JEREMY TAYLOR. By Miss SEWELL. 32mo. 3s.

Bishop Jeremy Taylor's Entire Works; with Life by BISHOP HEBER. Revised and corrected by the Rev. C. P EDEN. 10 vols. 8vo. price £5. 5s.

Traditions and Customs of Cathedrals. By MACKENZIE E. C. WALCOTT, B.D. F.S.A. Præcentor and Prebendary of Chichester. Second Edition, revised and enlarged. Crown 8vo. price 6s.

Spiritual Songs for the Sundays and Holidays throughout the Year. By J. S. B. MONSELL, LL.D. Vicar of Egham and Rural Dean. Fourth Edition, Sixth Thousand. Fcp. price 4s. 6d.

Lyra Germanica, translated from the German by Miss C. WINKWORTH. FIRST SERIES, the *Christian Year*, Hymns for the Sundays and Chief Festivals of the Church; SECOND SERIES, the *Christian Life*. Fcp. 8vo. price 3s. 6d. each SERIES.

Endeavours after the Christian Life; Discourses. By JAMES MARTINEAU. Fourth Edition. Post 8vo. price 7s. 6d.

Travels, Voyages, &c.

Rambles, by PATRICIUS WALKER. Reprinted from *Fraser's Magazine*; with a Vignette of the Queen's Bower, in the New Forest. Crown 8vo. price 10s. 6d.

Slave-Catching in the Indian Ocean; a Record of Naval Experiences. By Capt. COLOMB, R.N. 8vo. with Illustrations from Photographs, &c. price 21s.

The Cruise of H.M.S. Curaçoa among the South Sea Islands in 1865. By JULIUS BRENCHLEY, M.A. F.R.G.S. 8vo. with Map and Plates. [*Nearly ready.*

Six Months in California. By J.G. PLAYER-FROWD. Post 8vo. price 6s.

The Japanese in America. By CHARLES LANMAN, American Secretary, Japanese Legation, Washington, U.S.A. Post 8vo. price 10s. 6d.

My Wife and I in Queensland; Eight Years' Experience in the Colony, with some account of Polynesian Labour. By CHARLES H. EDEN. With Map and Frontispiece. Crown 8vo. price 9s.

Untrodden Peaks and Unfrequented Valleys; a Midsummer Ramble among the Dolomites. By AMELIA B. EDWARDS, Author of 'Barbara's History' &c. With a Map, and numerous Illustrations from Designs by the Author; Engraved on Wood by E. Whymper. Medium 8vo. uniform with Whymper's 'Scrambles in the Alps.' [*Nearly ready.*

How to See Norway. By Captain J. R. CAMPBELL. With Map and 5 Woodcuts. Fcp. 8vo. price 5s.

Pau and the Pyrenees. By Count HENRY RUSSELL, Member of the Alpine Club. With 2 Maps. Fcp. 8vo. price 5s.

Hours of Exercise in the Alps. By JOHN TYNDALL, LL.D., F.R.S. Third Edition, with Seven Woodcuts by E. Whymper. Crown 8vo. price 12s. 6d.

Cadore or Titian's Country. By JOSIAH GILBERT, one of the Authors of the 'Dolomite Mountains.' With Map, Facsimile, and 40 Illustrations. Imp. 8vo. 31s. 6d.

The Dolomite Mountains. Excursions through Tyrol, Carinthia, Carniola, and Friuli. By J. GILBERT and G. C. CHURCHILL, F.R.G.S. With numerous Illustrations. Square crown 8vo. 21s.

Travels in the Central Caucasus and Bashan, including Visits to Ararat and Tabreez and Ascents of Kazbek and Elbruz. By DOUGLAS W. FRESHFIELD. Square crown 8vo. with Maps, &c., 18s.

Life in India; a Series of Sketches shewing something of the Anglo-Indian, the Land he lives in, and the People among whom he lives. By EDWARD BRADDON. Post 8vo. price 9s.

The Alpine Club Map of the Chain of Mont Blanc, from an actual Survey in 1863—1864. By A. ADAMS-REILLY, F.R.G.S. M.A.C. In Chromolithography on extra stout drawing paper 28in. × 17in. price 10s. or mounted on canvas in a folding case, 12s. 6d.

History of Discovery in our Australasian Colonies, Australia, Tasmania, and New Zealand, from the Earliest Date to the Present Day. By WILLIAM HOWITT. 2 vols. 8vo. with 3 Maps, 20s.

Visits to Remarkable Places: Old Halls, Battle-Fields, and Scenes illustrative of striking Passages in English History and Poetry. By the same Author. 2 vols. square crown 8vo. with Wood Engravings, 25s.

The Rural Life of England. By WILLIAM HOWITT. Woodcuts by Bewick and Williams. Medium 8vo. 12s. 6d.

Guide to the Pyrenees, for the use of Mountaineers. By CHARLES PACKE. Second Edition, with Maps, &c. and Appendix. Crown 8vo. 7s. 6d.

The Alpine Guide. By JOHN BALL M.R.I.A. late President of the Alpine Club. Post 8vo. with Maps and other Illustrations.

The Guide to the Eastern Alps, price 10s. 6d.

The Guide to the Western Alps, including Mont Blanc, Monte Rosa, Zermatt, &c. Price 6s. 6d.

Guide to the Central Alps, including all the Oberland District, price 7s. 6d.

Introduction on Alpine Travelling in general, and on the Geology of the Alps, price 1s. Either of the Three Volumes or Parts of the *Alpine Guide* may be had with this INTRODUCTION prefixed, price 1s. extra.

Works of Fiction.

The Burgomaster's Family; or, Weal and Woe in a Little World. By CHRISTINE MÜLLER. Translated from the Dutch by Sir J. SHAW LEFEVRE, K.C.B. F.R.S. Crown 8vo. price 6s.

Popular Romances of the Middle Ages. By the Rev. GEORGE W. COX, M.A. and EUSTACE HINTON JONES. Crown 8vo. 10s. 6d.

Tales of the Teutonic Lands; a Sequel to 'Popular Romances of the Middle Ages.' By GEORGE W. COX, M.A. and EUSTACE HINTON JONES. Crown 8vo. price 10s. 6d.

Novels and Tales. By the Right Hon. BENJAMIN DISRAELI, M.P. Cabinet Editions, complete in Ten Volumes, crown 8vo. price 6s. each, as follows:—

LOTHAIR, 6s.	VENETIA, 6s.
CONINGSBY, 6s.	ALROY, IXION, &c. 6s.
SYBIL, 6s.	YOUNG DUKE, &c. 6s.
TANCRED, 6s.	VIVIAN GREY, 6s.
CONTARINI FLEMING, &c. 6s.	
HENRIETTA TEMPLE, 6s.	

Cabinet Edition, in crown 8vo. of Stories and Tales by Miss SEWELL:—

AMY HERBERT, 2s. 6d.	KATHARINE ASHTON, 2s. 6d.
GERTRUDE, 2s. 6d.	MARGARET PERCIVAL, 3s. 6d.
EARL'S DAUGHTER, 2s. 6d.	LANETON PARSONAGE, 3s. 6d.
EXPERIENCE of LIFE, 2s. 6d.	URSULA, 3s. 6d.
CLEVE HALL, 2s. 6d.	
IVORS, 2s. 6d.	

Becker's Gallus; or, Roman Scenes of the Time of Augustus. Post 8vo. 7s. 6d.

Becker's Charicles: Illustrative of Private Life of the Ancient Greeks. Post 8vo. 7s. 6d.

Tales of Ancient Greece. By the Rev. G. W. Cox, M.A. late Scholar of Trin. Coll. Oxford. Crown 8vo. price 6s. 6d.

Wonderful Stories from Norway, Sweden, and Iceland. Adapted and arranged by JULIA GODDARD. With an Introductory Essay by the Rev. G. W. COX, M.A. and Six Illustrations. Square post 8vo. 6s.

The Modern Novelist's Library:
MELVILLE'S DIGBY GRAND, 2s. boards; 2s. 6d. cloth.
———— GLADIATORS, 2s. boards; 2s. 6d. cloth.
———— GOOD FOR NOTHING, 2s. boards; 2s. 6d. cloth.
———— HOLMBY HOUSE, 2s. boards; 2s. 6d. cloth.
———— INTERPRETER, 2s. boards; 2s. 6d. cloth.
———— KATE COVENTRY, 2s. boards; 2s. 6d. cloth.
———— QUEEN'S MARIES, 2s. boards; 2s. 6d. cloth.
———— GENERAL BOUNCE, 2s. boards 2s. 6d. cloth.
TROLLOPE'S WARDEN 1s. 6d. boards; 2s cloth.
———— BARCHESTER TOWERS, 2s. boards; 2s. 6d. cloth.
BRAMLEY-MOORE'S SIX SISTERS OF THE VALLEYS, 2s. boards; 2s. 6d. cloth.

Poetry and The Drama.

Ballads and Lyrics of Old France; with other Poems. By A. LANG, Fellow of Merton College, Oxford. Square fcp. 8vo. price 5s.

Moore's Lalla Rookh, Tenniel's Edition, with 68 Wood Engravings from Original Drawings. Fcp. 4to. 21s.

Moore's Irish Melodies, Maclise's Edition, with 161 Steel Plates from Original Drawings. Super-royal 8vo. 31s. 6d.

Miniature Edition of Moore's Irish *Melodies*, with Maclise's Illustrations (as above), reduced in Lithography. Imp. 16mo. 10s. 6d.

Lays of Ancient Rome; with *Ivry* and the *Armada*. By the Right Hon. LORD MACAULAY. 16mo. 3s. 6d.

Lord Macaulay's Lays of Ancient Rome. With 90 Illustrations on Wood, Original and from the Antique, from Drawings by G. SCHARF. Fcp. 4to. 21s.

Miniature Edition of Lord Macaulay's Lays of Ancient Rome, with Scharf's Illustrations (as above) reduced in Lithography. Imp. 16mo. 10s. 6d.

Southey's Poetical Works, with the Author's last Corrections and Copyright Additions. Library Edition. Medium 8vo. with Portrait and Vignette, 14s.

Goldsmith's Poetical Works, Illustrated with Wood Engravings from Designs by Members of the ETCHING CLUB. Imp. 16mo. 7s. 6d.

Poems. By JEAN INGELOW. 2 vols. Fcp. 8vo. price 10s.
FIRST SERIES, containing 'DIVIDED,' 'The STAR'S MONUMENT,' &c. Sixteenth Thousand. Fcp. 8vo. price 5s.
SECOND SERIES, 'A STORY of DOOM,' 'GLADYS and her ISLAND,' &c. Fifth Thousand. Fcp. 8vo. price 5s.

Poems by Jean Ingelow. First Series, with nearly 100 Illustrations engraved on Wood. Fcp. 4to. 21s.

Bowdler's Family Shakspeare cheaper Genuine Edition, complete in 1 vol. large type, with 36 Woodcut Illustrations, price 14s. or in 6 pocket vols. 3s. 6d. each.

Horatii Opera, Library Edition, with Copious English Notes, Marginal References and Various Readings. Edited by the Rev. J. E. YONGE, M.A. 8vo. 21s.

The Odes and Epodes of Horace; a Metrical Translation into English, with Introduction and Commentaries. By Lord LYTTON. Post 8vo. price 10s. 6d.

The Æneid of Virgil Translated into English Verse. By the late J. CONINGTON, M.A. New Edition. Crown 8vo. 9s.

Rural Sports &c.

Encyclopædia of Rural Sports; a Complete Account, Historical, Practical, and Descriptive, of Hunting, Shooting, Fishing, Racing, &c. By D. P. BLAINE. With above 600 Woodcuts (20 from Designs by JOHN LEECH). 8vo. 21s.

The Dead Shot, or Sportsman's Complete Guide; a Treatise on the Use of the Gun, Dog-breaking, Pigeon-shooting, &c. By MARKSMAN. Fcp. 8vo. with Plates, 5s.

A Book on Angling: being a Complete Treatise on the Art of Angling in every branch, including full Illustrated Lists of Salmon Flies. By FRANCIS FRANCIS. New Edition, with Portrait and 15 other Plates, plain and coloured. Post 8vo. 15s.

Wilcocks's Sea-Fisherman: comprising the Chief Methods of Hook and Line Fishing in the British and other Seas, a glance at Nets, and remarks on Boats and Boating. Second Edition, enlarged, with 80 Woodcuts. Post 8vo. 12s. 6d.

The Fly-Fisher's Entomology. By ALFRED RONALDS. With coloured Representations of the Natural and Artificial Insect. Sixth Edition, with 20 coloured Plates. 8vo. 14s.

The Ox, his Diseases and their Treatment; with an Essay on Parturition in the Cow. By J. R. DOBSON, M.R.C.V.S. Crown 8vo. with Illustrations, 7s. 6d.

A Treatise on Horse-shoeing and Lameness. By JOSEPH GAMGEE, Veterinary Surgeon, formerly Lecturer on the Principles and Practice of Farriery in the New Veterinary College, Edinburgh. 8vo. with 55 Woodcuts, 15s.

Blaine's Veterinary Art: a Treatise on the Anatomy, Physiology, and Curative Treatment of the Diseases of the Horse, Neat Cattle, and Sheep. Seventh Edition, revised and enlarged by C. STEEL. 8vo. with Plates and Woodcuts, 18s.

Youatt on the Horse. Revised and enlarged by W. WATSON, M.R.C.V.S. 8vo. with numerous Woodcuts, 12s. 6d.

Youatt on the Dog. By the same Author. 8vo. with numerous Woodcuts price 6s.

Horses and Stables. By Colonel F. FITZWYGRAM, XV. the King's Hussars. With 24 Plates of Woodcut Illustrations, containing very numerous Figures. 8vo. 15s.

The Dog in Health and Disease. By STONEHENGE. With 73 Wood Engravings. New Edition, revised. Square crown 8vo. price 7s. 6d.

The Greyhound. By the same Author. Revised Edition, with 24 Portraits of Greyhounds. Square crown 8vo. 10s. 6d.

Stables and Stable Fittings. By W.MILES,Esq. Imp. 8vo. with 13 Plates, 15s.

The Horse's Foot, and how to keep it Sound. By W. MILES, Esq. Ninth Edition, with Illustrations. Imp. 8vo. 12s. 6d.

A Plain Treatise on Horse-shoeing. By the same Author. Sixth Edition, post 8vo. with Illustrations, 2s. 6d.

Remarks on Horses' Teeth, addressed to Purchasers. By the same. Post 8vo. 1s. 6d.

The Setter; with Notices of the most Eminent Breeds now extant, Instructions how to Breed, Rear, and Break; Dog Shows, Field Trials, and General Management, &c. By EDWARD LAVERACK. With 2 Portraits of Setters. Crown 4to. 7s. 6d.

Works of Utility and General Information.

Chess Openings. By F. W. LONGMAN, Balliol College, Oxford. Fcp. 8vo. 2s. 6d.

The Theory of the Modern Scientific Game of Whist. By WILLIAM POLE, F.R.S. Mus. Doc. Oxon. Fifth Edition, enlarged. Fcp. 8vo. price 2s. 6d.

A Practical Treatise on Brewing; with Formulæ for Public Brewers, and Instructions for Private Families. By W BLACK. Fifth Edition. 8vo. 10s. 6d.

The Theory and Practice of Banking. By HENRY DUNNING MACLEOD, M.A. Barrister-at-Law. Second Edition. entirely remodelled. 2 vols. 8vo. 30s.

Collieries and Colliers: a Handbook of the Law and Leading Cases relating thereto. By J. C. FOWLER, Barrister. Third Edition. Fcp. 8vo. 7s. 6d.

Modern Cookery for Private Families, reduced to a System of Easy Practice in a Series of carefully-tested Receipts. By ELIZA ACTON. Newly revised and enlarged; with 8 Plates, Figures, and 150 Woodcuts. Fcp. 6s.

Maunder's Treasury of Knowledge and Library of Reference: comprising an English Dictionary and Grammar, Universal Gazetteer, Classical Dictionary, Chronology, Law Dictionary, Synopsis of the Peerage, Useful Tables, &c. Fcp. 8vo. 6s.

Pewtner's Comprehensive Specifier; a Guide to the Practical Specification of every kind of Building-Artificer's Work: with Forms of Building Conditions and Agreements, an Appendix, Foot-Notes, and Index. Edited by W. YOUNG, Architect. Crown 8vo. 6s.

M'Culloch's Dictionary, Practical, Theoretical, and Historical, of Commerce and Commercial Navigation. New Edition, revised throughout and corrected to the Present Time; with a Biographical Notice of the Author. Edited by H. G. REID. 8vo. price 63s.

Hints to Mothers on the Management of their Health during the Period of Pregnancy and in the Lying-in Room. By THOMAS BULL, M.D. Fcp. 8vo. price 5s.

The Maternal Management of Children in Health and Disease. By THOMAS BULL, M.D. Fcp. 8vo. price 5s.

How to Nurse Sick Children; containing Directions which may be found of service to all who have charge of the Young. By CHARLES WEST, M.D. Second Edition. Fcp. 8vo. 1s. 6d

Notes on Lying-In Institutions; with a Proposal for Organising an Institution for Training Midwives and Midwifery Nurses. By FLORENCE NIGHTINGALE. With 5 Plans. Square crown 8vo. 7s. 6d.

Blackstone Economised; being a Compendium of the Laws of England to the Present Time. By D. M. AIRD, of the Middle Temple, Barrister-at-Law. Post 8vo. 7s. 6d.

The Cabinet Lawyer; a Popular Digest of the Laws of England, Civil, Criminal, and Constitutional. Twenty-third Edition, corrected and brought up to the Present Date. Fcp. 8vo. price 7s. 6d.

A Profitable Book upon Domestic Law. Essays for English Women and Law Students. By PERKINS, Junior, M.A. Barrister-at-Law. Post 8vo. price 10s. 6d.

A History and Explanation of the Stamp Duties; containing Remarks on the Origin of the Stamp Duties and a History of the Stamp Duties in this Country from their Commencement to the Present Time. By STEPHEN DOWELL, M.A. Assistant-Solicitor of Inland Revenue. 8vo. price 12s. 6d.

Willich's Popular Tables for Ascertaining the Value of Lifehold, Leasehold, and Church Property, Renewal Fines, &c. with numerous useful Chemical, Geographical, Astronomical, Trigonometrical Tables, &c. Post 8vo. 10s.

INDEX.

ACTON's Modern Cookery 20
AIRD's Blackstone Economised 20
ALLIES on Formation of Christendom 16
ALLEN's Discourses of Chrysostom 16
Alpine Guide (The) 18
AMOS's Jurisprudence 5
ANDERSON's Strength of Materials 9
ARNOLD's Manual of English Literature .. 6
Authority and Conscience 15
Autumn Holidays of a Country Parson 7
AYRE's Treasury of Bible Knowledge...... 16

BACON's Essays by WHATELY 5
───── Life and Letters, by SPEDDING .. 4
───── Works............................ 5
BAIN's Mental and Moral Science 8
───── on the Senses and Intellect 8
BALL's Guide to the Central Alps.......... 18
───── Guide to the Western Alps 18
───── Guide to the Eastern Alps 18
BAYLDON's Rents and Tillages .... •15
BECKER's *Charicles* and *Gallus* 18
BENFEY's Sanskrit-English Dictionary 6
BLACK's Treatise on Brewing.............. 20
BLACKLEY's German-English Dictionary .. 6
BLAINE's Rural Sports 19
───── Veterinary Art 19
BLOXAM's Metals......................... 9
BOOTH's Problem of the World and the Church 15
───── Saint-Simon 3
BOULTBEE on 39 Articles 15
BOURNE's Catechism of the Steam Engine.. 14
───── Handbook of Steam Engine 14
───── Treatise on the Steam Engine.... 14
───── Improvements in the same 14
BOWDLER's Family SHAKSPEARE........... 19
BRADDON's Life in India 17
BRAMLEY-MOORE's Six Sisters of the Valley 18
BRANDE's Dictionary of Science, Literature, and Art.................................. 11
BRAY's Manual of Anthropology 8
───── Philosophy of Necessity 8
───── On Force 8
BREE's Fallacies of Darwinism 11
BRENCHLEY's Cruise of the 'Curaçoa' 17
BROWNE's Exposition of the 39 Articles.... 16
BRUNEL's Life of BRUNEL 4
BUCKLE's History of Civilisation 2
───── Posthumous Remains 7
BULL's Hints to Mothers 20
───── Maternal Management of Children.. 20
BUNSEN's God in History.................. 3
───── Prayers 15
Burgomaster's Family (The) 18
BURKE's Rise of Great Families 5
───── Vicissitudes of Families.......... 5

BURTON's Christian Church 3

Cabinet Lawyer........................... 20
CAMPBELL's Norway 17
CATES's Biographical Dictionary 4
───── and WOODWARD's Encyclopædia 2
CATS and FARLIE's Moral Emblems 13
Changed Aspects of Unchanged Truths 7
CHESNEY's Indian Polity 2
───── Waterloo Campaign 2
Chorale Book for England 13
Christ the Consoler....................... 15
CLOUGH's Lives from Plutarch 2
CODRINGTON's (Admiral) Memoirs........ 4
COLENSO on Pentateuch and Book of Joshua 16
───── The Speaker's Bible Commentary 15
COLLINS's Perspective 14
COLOMB's Slave Catching in the Indian Ocean 17
Commonplace Philosopher in Town and Country, by A. K. H. B. 7
CONINGTON's Translation of Virgil's Æneid 19
───── Miscellaneous Writings 7
CONTANSEAU's Two French Dictionaries.. 6
CONYBEARE and HOWSON's Life and Epistles of St. Paul 16
COOKE's Grotesque Animals 13
COOPER's Surgical Dictionary.............. 12
COPLAND's Dictionary of Practical Medicine 13
COTTON's Memoir and Correspondence 4
Counsel and Comfort from a City Pulpit .. 7
Cox's (G. W.) Aryan Mythology 3
───── History of Greece 2
───── Tale of the Great Persian War 2
───── Tales of Ancient Greece 18
───── and JONES's Romances...... 18
───── Teutonic Tales.. 18
CREASY on British Constitution 2
CRESY's Encyclopædia of Civil Engineering 14
Critical Essays of a Country Parson........ 7
CROOKES on Beet-Root Sugar.............. 15
───── 's Chemical Analysis.............. 12
CULLEY's Handbook of Telegraphy 14
CUSACK's Student's History of Ireland 2

DAVIDSON's Introduction to New Testament 16
Dead Shot (The), by MARKSMAN 19
DE CAISNE and LE MAOUT's Botany 11
DE MORGAN's Paradoxes 7
DENISON's Vice-Regal Life 1
DISRAELI's Lord George Bentinck 4
───── Novels and Tales 19
DOBSON on the Ox 19
DOVE's Law of Storms 9
DOWELL on Stamp Duties 20
DOYLE's Fairyland 13
DREW's Reasons of Faith 13

NEW WORKS PUBLISHED BY LONGMANS AND CO.

EASTLAKE'S Gothic Revival 14
—— Hints on Household Taste 14
EATON'S Musical Criticism and Biography 4
EDEN'S Queensland...................... 17
EDWARDS'S Rambles among the Dolomites 17
Elements of Botany 11
ELLICOTT'S Commentary on Ephesians 16
—————————— Galatians 16
—————————— Pastoral Epist. 16
—————————— Philippians,&c. 16
—————————— Thessalonians 16
—————'s Lectures on Life of Christ 16
ERICHSEN'S Surgery 12
EVANS'S Ancient Stone Implements 11
EWALD'S History of Israel 16

FAIRBAIRN'S Application of Cast and Wrought Iron to Building 14
————— Information for Engineers.... 14
————— Treatise on Mills and Millwork 14
FARADAY'S Life and Letters 4
FITZWYGRAM on Horses and Stables 20
FOWLER'S Collieries and Colliers 20
FRANCIS'S Fishing Book 19
FRESHFIELD'S Travels in the Caucasus 17
FROUDE'S English in Ireland 1
——— History of England 1
——— Short Studies 7

GAMGEE on Horse-Shoeing 19
GANOT'S Elementary Physics 9
——— Natural Philosophy 9
GARROD'S Materia Medica 13
GILBERT'S Cadore 17
———— and CHURCHILL'S Dolomites 17
GIRDLESTONE'S Bible Synonyms 15
GIRTIN'S House I Live In 12
GLEDSTONE'S Life of WHITEFIELD 4
GODDARD'S Wonderful Stories 18
GOLDSMITH'S Poems, Illustrated 19
GOODEVE'S Mechanism.................... 9
GRAHAM'S Autobiography of MILTON...... 4
——— View of Literature and Art 2
GRANT'S Ethics of Aristotle............ 5
Graver Thoughts of a Country Parson..... 7
Gray's Anatomy......................... 12
GREENHOW on Bronchitis 12
GRIFFIN'S Algebra and Trigonometry 9
GRIFFITH'S Fundamentals 15
GROVE on Correlation of Physical Forces .. 9
GURNEY'S Chapters of French History 2
GWILT'S Encyclopædia of Architecture 14

HARE on Election of Representatives..... 7
HARTWIG'S Aerial World................. 10
————— Harmonies of Nature.......... 10
————— Polar World 10
————— Sea and its Living Wonders.... 10
————— Subterranean World 10
————— Tropical World 10
HATHERTON'S Memoir and Correspondence 2
HAUGHTON'S Animal Mechanics 10
HAYWARD'S Biographical and Critical Essays 4
HELMHOLTZ'S Scientific Lectures......... 9
HEMSLEY'S Trees, Shrubs, and Herbaceous Pants................................ 11
HERSCHEL'S Outlines of Astronomy........ 8

HEWITT on the Diseases of Women .... 1?
HODGSON'S Time and Space................ ?
——— Theory of Practice .... ?
HOLLAND'S Recollections................. 4
HOLMES'S Surgical Treatment of Children.. 1?
——— System of Surgery .... 1?
HOWITT'S Australian Discovery........... 16
——— Rural Life of England 16
——— Visits to Remarkable Places 16
HÜBNER'S Pope Sixtus the Fifth 4
HUMBOLDT'S Life......................... 4
HUME'S Essays .... ?
——— Treatise on Human Nature........ ?

IHNE'S History of Rome .... ?
INGELOW'S Poems .... 1?

JAMES'S Christian Counsels.............. 1?
JAMESON'S Legends of Saints and Martyrs.. 1?
——— Legends of the Madonna ...... 1?
——— Legends of the Monastic Orders 1?
——— Legends of the Saviour......... 1?
JAMIESON on Causality................... ?
JARDINE'S Christian Sacerdotalism ...... 1?
JOHNSTON'S Geographical Dictionary ...... ?

KALISCH'S Commentary on the Bible...... ?
KEITH on Destiny of the World........... 1?
——— Fulfilment of Prophecy.......... 1?
KENYON'S (Lord) Life¹................... 4
KERL'S Metallurgy, by CROOKES and ROHRIG .... 1?
KIRBY and SPENCE'S Entomology.......... 1?

LANG'S Ballads and Lyrics .... 1?
LANMAN'S Japanese in America .... 1?
LATHAM'S English Dictionary............. ?
LAUGHTON'S Nautical Surveying........... ?
LAVERACK'S Setters .... 2?
LECKY'S History of European Morals ...... ?
——— Rationalism............. ?
——— Leaders of Public Opinion.. ...... ?
Leisure Hours in Town, by A. K. H. B. .... ?
Lessons of Middle Age, by A. K. H. B. .... ?
LEWES'S Biographical History of Philosophy ?
LIDDELL & SCOTT'S Greek-English Lexicons ?
Life of Man Symbolised.................. 1?
LINDLEY and MOORE'S Treasury of Botany 1?
LONGMAN'S Edward the Third .... ?
——— Lectures on History of England ?
——— Chess Openings................ 2?
LOUDON'S Encyclopædia of Agriculture .... 1?
——— Gardening ...... 1?
——— Plants .... 1?
LUBBOCK'S Origin of Civilisation .... 1?
LYTTON'S Odes of Horace................. 1?
Lyra Germanica .... 13, 1?

MACAULAY'S (Lord) Essays .... ?
——— History of England .. ?
——— Lays of Ancient Rome 1?
——— Miscellaneous Writings ?
——— Speeches .... ?
——— Works .... ?
MACLEOD'S Principles of Economical Philosophy ....

MACLEOD'S Dictionary of Political Economy	5
———————— Theory and Practice of Banking	20
MCCULLOCH'S Dictionary of Commerce	20
Mankind, their Origin and Destiny	11
MANNING'S England and Christendom	16
MARCET'S Natural Philosophy	9
MARSHALL'S Physiology	13
MARSHMAN'S History of India	2
———————— Life of Havelock	
MARTINEAU'S Endeavours after the Christian Life	17
MASSINGBERD'S History of the Reformation	3
MATHEWS on Colonial Question	2
MAUNDER'S Biographical Treasury	5
———————— Geographical Treasury	9
———————— Historical Treasury	3
———————— Scientific and Literary Treasury	11
———————— Treasury of Knowledge	20
———————— Treasury of Natural History	11
MAXWELL'S Theory of Heat	9
MAY'S Constitutional History of England	1
MELVILLE'S Digby Grand	18
———————— General Bounce	18
———————— Gladiators	18
———————— Good for Nothing	18
———————— Holmby House	18
———————— Interpreter	18
———————— Kate Coventry	18
———————— Queen's Maries	18
MENDELSSOHN'S Letters	4
MERIVALE'S Fall of the Roman Republic	2
———————— Romans under the Empire	2
MERRIFIELD'S Arithmetic and Mensuration	9
———————— Magnetism	8
MILES on Horse's Foot and Horse Shoeing	20
——— on Horses' Teeth and Stables	20
MILL (J.) on the Mind	5
MILL (J. S.) on Liberty	5
———————— Subjection of Women	5
———————— on Representative Government	5
———————— on Utilitarianism	5
———————'s Dissertations and Discussions	5
———————— Political Economy	5
———————— System of Logic	5
———————— Hamilton's Philosophy	5
MILLER'S Elements of Chemistry	11
———————— Inorganic Chemistry	9
MITCHELL'S Manual of Architecture	14
———————— Manual of Assaying	14
MONSELL'S 'Spiritual Songs'	17
MOORE'S Irish Melodies, illustrated	19
———————— Lalla Rookh, illustrated	19
MORELL'S Elements of Psychology	7
———————— Mental Philosophy	7
MOSSMAN'S Christian Church	3
MÜLLER'S Chips from a German Workshop	7
———————— Science of Language	6
———————— Science of Religion	3
MURCHISON on Liver Complaints	13
———————— on Continued Fevers	13
NASH'S Compendium of the Prayer-Book	15
New Testament Illustrated with Wood Engravings from the Old Masters	13
NEWMAN'S Apologia pro Vitâ Suâ	5
NIGHTINGALE on Lying-In Institutions	20
NILSSON'S Scandinavia	10
NORTHCOTT on Lathes and Turning	14
O'CONNOR'S Commentary on Hebrews	16
———————— Romans	16

ODLING'S Course of Practical Chemistry	11
OWEN'S Comparative Anatomy and Physiology of Vertebrate Animals	10
———————— Lectures on the Invertebrata	10
PACKE'S Guide to the Pyrenees	18
PAGET'S Lectures on Surgical Pathology	12
PEREIRA'S Elements of Materia Medica	13
PERKIN'S Profitable Book on Domestic Law	20
PERRING'S Churches and Creeds	15
PEWTNER'S Comprehensive Specifier	20
PLAYER-FROWD'S California	17
POLE'S Game of Whist	20
PRENDERGAST'S Mastery of Languages	6
PRESCOTT'S Scripture Difficulties	16
Present-Day Thoughts, by A. K. H. B.	7
PROCTOR'S Astronomical Essays	8
———————— Orbs around Us	8
———————— Plurality of Worlds	8
———————— Saturn	8
———————— Scientific Essays	10
———————— Star Atlas	9
———————— Star Depths	8
———————— Sun	8
Public Schools Atlas	9
QUAIN'S Anatomy	12
RANKEN on Strains in Trusses	14
RAWLINSON'S Parthia	2
Recreations of a Country Parson, by A. K. H. B.	7
REEVE'S Royal and Republican France	2
REICHEL'S See of Rome	14
REILLY'S Map of Mont Blanc	18
RICH'S Dictionary of Antiquities	6
RIVERS'S Rose Amateur's Guide	11
ROGERS'S Eclipse of Faith	7
———————— Defence of Eclipse of Faith	7
ROGET'S Thesaurus of English Words and Phrases	6
RONALDS'S Fly-Fisher's Entomology	19
ROSE'S Loyola	16
ROTHSCHILD'S Israelites	16
RUSSELL'S Pau and the Pyrenees	17
RUSSELL (Earl) on the Rise and Progress of the Christian Religion	3
SANDARS'S Justinian's Institutes	5
SANFORD'S English Kings	1
SAVORY'S Geometric Turning	14
SCHELLEN'S Spectrum Analysis	8
SCOTT'S Lectures on the Fine Arts	13
———————— Albert Durer	13
Seaside Musing, by A. K. H. B.	7
SEEBOHM'S Oxford Reformers of 1498	2
SEWELL'S History of the Early Church	3
———————— Passing Thoughts on Religion	16
———————— Preparation for Communion	17
———————— Readings for Confirmation	17
———————— Readings for Lent	17
———————— Examination for Confirmation	17
———————— Stories and Tales	18
———————— Thoughts for the Age	16
———————— Thoughts for the Holy Week	17
SHIPLEY'S Essays on Ecclesiastical Reform	15
SHORT'S Church History	3

SMITH's Paul's Voyage and Shipwreck 16
—— (SYDNEY) Life and Letters 4
—————— Miscellaneous Works .. 7
—————— Wit and Wisdom 7
—— (Dr. Hy.) Handbook for Midwives 12
—— (Dr. R. A.) Air and Rain 8
SOUTHEY's Doctor 6
—————— Poetical Works................ 19
STANLEY': History of British Birds........ 10
STEPHEN's Ecclesiastical Biography 4
STIRLING's Philosophy of Law 7
—————— Protoplasm................. 8
—————— Secret of Hegel............... 7
—————— Sir WILLIAM HAMILTON...... 8
STOCKMAR's Memoirs 1
STONEHENGE on the Dog................... 20
—————— on the Greyhound 20
STRICKLAND's Queens of England 5
STUART-GLENNIE's Morningland......... 7
Sunday Afternoons at the Parish Church of
a University City, by A. K. H. B. 7

TAYLOR's History of India 2
—————— (Jeremy) Works, edited by EDEN 17
Text-Books of Science 9
THIRLWALL's History of Greece 2
THOMSON's Laws of Thought 5
THUDICHUM's Chemical Physiology 12
TODD (A.) on Parliamentary Government .. 1
—————— and BOWMAN's Anatomy and Physiology of Man 13
TRENCH's Realities of Irish Life 2
TROLLOPE's Barchester Towers............ 18
—————— Warden 18
TYNDALL's American Lectures on Light.... 10
—————— Diamagnetism 10
—————— Faraday as a Discoverer........ 4
—————— Fragments of Science......... 9
—————— Hours of Exercise in the Alps.. 17
—————— Lectures on Electricity 10
—————— Lectures on Light 10
—————— Lectures on Sound 10
—————— Heat a Mode of Motion 10
—————— Molecular Physics 11

UEBERWEG's System of Logic 8

URE's Dictionary of Arts, Manufactures, and
Mines 14

VOGAN's Doctrine of the Eucharist 15

WALCOTT's Traditions of Cathedrals 17
WALKER's (PATRICIUS) Rambles.......... 17
WATSON's Geometry 9
—————— Principles and Practice of Physic 12
WATTS's Dictionary of Chemistry.......... 11
WEBB's Objects for Common Telescopes.... 9
WEBSTER & WILKINSON's Greek Testament 16
WEINHOLD's Experimental Physics........ 9
WELLINGTON's Life, by GLEIG 4
WEST on Children's Diseases 12
—————— on Children's Nervous Disorders 12
—————— on Nursing Sick Children 20
WHATELY's English Synonymes 5
—————— Logic 5
—————— Rhetoric..................... 5
WHITE and RIDDLE's Latin Dictionaries .. 6
WILCOCKS's Sea Fisherman................ 19
WILLIAMS's Aristotle's Ethics 5
WILLIAMS on Climate 12
—————— on Consumption 12
WILLICH's Popular Tables 20
WILLIS's Principles of Mechanism 14
WINSLOW on Light....................... 10
WOOD's (J. G.) Bible Animals.............. 11
—————— Homes without Hands 10
—————— Insects at Home 10
—————— Insects Abroad 10
—————— Strange Dwellings 10
—————— (T.) Chemical Notes 12
WORDSWORTH's Christian Ministry........ 15

YONGE's History of England 1
—————— English-Greek Lexicons 6
—————— Horace 19
—————— English Literature................ 6
—————— Modern History 8
YOUATT on the Dog 20
—————— on the Horse................... 20

ZELLER's Socrates 3
—————— Stoics, Epicureans, and Sceptics.. 3

SPOTTISWOODE AND CO., PRINTERS, NEW-STREET SQUARE, LONDON.

www.ingramcontent.com/pod-product-compliance
Lightning Source LLC
Chambersburg PA
CBHW032244080426
42735CB00008B/999